THE COOPER AND
HIS TRADE

THE
COOPER
AND HIS
TRADE

KENNETH
KILBY

LINDEN PUBLISHING CO., INC.
FRESNO, CALIFORNIA 93726

© 1971 KENNETH KILBY

FIRST PUBLISHED 1971 REPRINTED 1977
JOHN BAKER PUBLISHERS LTD
SUBSIDIARY COMPANY OF A & C BLACK PLC
LONDON

ISBN: 0-941936-16-3

Kilby, Kenneth.
   The cooper and his trade / Kenneth Kilby.
     p.   cm.
   Reprint. Originally published: London : J. Baker, 1971
   Includes bibliographical references.
   ISBN 0-941936-16-3
   1. Coopers and cooperage. 2. Coopers and cooperage—History.
I. Title.
TS890.K53   1989
674'.82—dc20   89-14518
                                          CIP

LINDEN PUBLISHING CO. INC.
3845 N. BLACKSTONE
FRESNO, CALIFORNIA 93726

Contents

Illustrations

PLATES

FIGURES

Introduction

So much has been written in the history books of kings and causes that we are apt to lose sight of the day-to-day job of living, the way of life of ordinary people, the very basis of that wealth without which kings would look ridiculous and causes superfluous. I would like to stake a claim for a place in history for the band of ordinary people, men who worked with the skill of their hands and the sweat of their brow, of tradesmen who have a history longer than any dynasty or house of kings, who know no frontiers in the practice of their craft and whose position in life is quite humble. In this country today there are now very few, not a 'happy few', as apart from one relatively small branch the trade is finished. I am writing about the Coopers, the trade whose name will be perpetuated in the surnames of people scattered across the world long after most people have forgotten what a barrel looked like. It was a wonderfully proud and honoured trade, aware of its monopoly of certain skills that became more and more in demand as world commerce expanded. It was a trade fiercely jealous of its good name, an organized, intensely loyal trade, which fought to safeguard its standards as well as its rewards. From its ranks have come pioneers of the Trade Union Movement, men who were prepared to take a stand against the law when they considered it to be unjust. In writing this book I was often reminded of Shakespeare's

> the evil that men do lives after them,
> the good is oft interred with their bones . . .

and thought that perhaps the coopers must have been a saintly company, but I seem to have found quite a quantity of information which makes them no better or worse than their fellows.

Part One
THE LIFE OF A CRAFTSMAN

CHAPTER ONE

The Making of a Cooper

Robinson Crusoe was able to make practically anything, but he never made a barrel. There are no amateur barrel-makers. Coopering is a skill acquired through years of sweating, muscle-aching, back-breaking labour 'at the block', as the coopers say. It is a rather conservative trade and proud of its traditions. Sons have followed fathers into the trade, and its secrets have been passed on from father to son for thousands of years. It's a family trade. Mr Alan Hall, the head of one of the largest cooperages in this country and still making casks for the whisky distillers, the only surviving coopering of any note, can boast that both his grandfathers were master coopers. Similarly with the Wilsons, the Roberts, the Oldhams, the Burmans, the Pettengells, the Novics, the Smiths and a host of others who have now put down their tools; it was in their blood. So it was with me. When I left school at Easter 1941, at the age of fourteen, it was natural that I, like my fathers before me, should become a cooper. My father had been a cooper all his life, serving his apprenticeship at Banbury in the cooper's shop of Samuel Kilby and Sons, his great-uncle and cousins. He had served as a cooper in the Navy on board the cruiser *Weymouth* during the Great War, when coopering was still a naval trade. His two brothers, my uncles, were both coopers. Mark, the younger brother, was killed at Ypres in 1917. He had a blazing row with Fred Kilby, Sam's son, threw down his tools and volunteered for the army. The older brother, William, worked for many years until his retirement, at Benskin's Brewery, Watford. His son Colin, my cousin, also took up the trade, working at Benskin's Brewery for some years after his apprenticeship, but left to take up the ministry and become a priest in the East End of London. My grandfather became a bound apprentice to Sam Kilby on 4 January 1877; a copy of his indentures is at fig. 84. He worked tremendously hard, coopering from early morning to nightfall at the block, and for a time set up on his own, where he might well have established himself, had not his capacity for hard work been exceeded by an even greater capacity for hard drinking. He was still working 'piecework' at the block in his seventies, and died at the ripe old age of ninety-eight. His uncle, Sam Kilby, set up his cooperage in North Bar, Banbury, the continuance of the Horse Fair, that very wide main road which leads away from the Cross towards Warwick and Stratford, in the year 1863. By the turn of the century he was employing upwards of thirty coopers at his cooperage in the Southam Road. On his death in 1903 the business passed to his son Fred, a very tall, well-built man with massive hands, a teetotaller and non-smoker who was profoundly religious. He was a 'big chapel man' and would often be heard singing a hymn as he walked along. Alongside the cooperage he set up a mineral-water factory. My father told me how, as an apprentice sweating away on a hot-afternoon under the galvanized iron roof of the cooperage, he had often nipped into the mineral-water factory, secreted one or two bottles in his apron, and made his way back to his block to hide them in among the shavings for future reference. It was on one of these escapades that he was abruptly halted by the strains of 'Rock of Ages', which gave him warning from above, and sufficient time to avoid capture. On Fred's death in 1936 the cooperage passed to his two sons, Ray and Frank. The business continued without any modernization until the early 1950s competing successfully against machine cooperages. It was then that the competition of metal barrels, bulk beer tanks, bottles and cans incorporated in new methods, and rising costs caused the bottom to drop out of the market for wooden barrels, and together with other cooperages the firm closed down. So much for the Kilby tradition.

In 1941 a boy leaving school at the age of fourteen had far more opportunities than a boy leaving school in the early thirties. The factories on war work were crying out for people, and apprenticeships in engineering were being offered to any boys who seriously sought them. However, at the back of most people's minds were memories of the aftermath of the first Great War and the subsequent unemployment, and people thought that as soon as the war was over there would again be widespread unemployment in the engineering industries, and were consequently wary of advising a boy to take up any form of engineering. 'They've always had barrels; they've always needed coopers, and they always will; you can depend on that', was the advice given to me in 1941. Within a quarter of a century these words were to be proved completely false.

I started work in the cooper's shop at J. W. Green's Brewery in Park

Street West, Luton, as an apprentice to my father, to work from 7.30 in the morning until 5.30 in the evening, from Monday to Friday, and from 8.0 until noon on Saturdays, for fifteen shillings a week, rising annually by ten shillings a week until I reached the age of twenty-one. And in the grimy, sooty cooperage, tucked away behind the chapel where the men were issued with their bever beer at eleven o'clock— Bever Time—I learned how to make a barrel. A barrel is, in fact, a particular size of wooden cask, one holding 36 gallons, and other sizes of casks go under different names.

At the age of fourteen a boy is not strong enough to perform many of the jobs done in coopering, even if he had the skill, and so I was given the more menial tasks to do. I swept up the shavings and kept the fire in. I loved the job of branding casks with a number, and underneath the name of the brewers, 'Green, Luton'. The smell of burning oak as the hot iron sinks into the timber is quite pleasant. We never had a ham or side of bacon hanging up in the chimney corner, as many cooperages used to have in earlier centuries, to become impregnated with the oak smoke; but my clothes acquired that aroma attributed

1. Painting and branding casks.

to the real old Harris tweed, the smoked smell, and I likewise. Another job I was given to do was that of painting the casks on each weather end, around the chime (fig. 1). If a cask stands on its end for any length of time, on earth or in water, then it is likely to rot, and for this reason, and in order to seal the end grain where some oaks, particularly English, tend to be occasionally porous, the chime is painted. As a primer we used to mix our own red and white lead powder with raw linseed oil and turpentine, and on top of this put an under- and a top-coat of malachite green, the brewery's colours. My father was very proud of the appearance of his casks and insisted upon neatness; J. W. Green's casks were as good as any in the country.

I was very soon given the job of boring the tap and bung holes into the casks, and fitting the brass bushes. Before you can bore the bung hole you have to find the centre of the cask, and to do this the cooper picks up one of the many pieces of 'flag' that litter the floor in a cooperage. 'Flag' is the name coopers use for the river rush which is specially harvested for them, and used for sealing joints in the casks, by reason of the fact that rush will swell when it comes into contact with water, and seal a slightly open joint. You take a flag about half the length of the cask, hold a piece of chalk to one end and measure the same distance to the centre from both ends, so that in the centre of where the chalk marks lie that is the centre of the cask. If a hole is not bored exactly in the centre, then the nozzle of the cask-washing machine, which squirts steam, and hot and cold water, or liquor as it is called in a brewery, into the cask, will not locate, and then there'd be trouble. The first hole is bored with an auger, and a taper is given to the hole with a tapered auger. Before screwing in the brass bush we always tied a piece of tarred yarn round the threads and wetted it with raw linseed oil; my father swore by this, an old naval knack, and believed that it stopped the wood from rotting. The bung stave is the weakest part of the cask, having a 2 in. hole cut into the very centre, and it is hammered every time a bung is inserted, so that it tends to crack rather more often than other staves, called side staves, to differentiate them from bung staves. We always chose as tough a stave as we could to fulfil the role of bung stave. Some coopers would bore the bung hole in between two staves, believing this to be a stronger job, but invariably one of the staves would prove to be slightly tougher than the other, which would give, and cause the cooper even more work than the one-stave bung. The tap-hole bush was fitted in a similar way into the key-stone cant, which is the piece of wood on one side of the top head oppo-

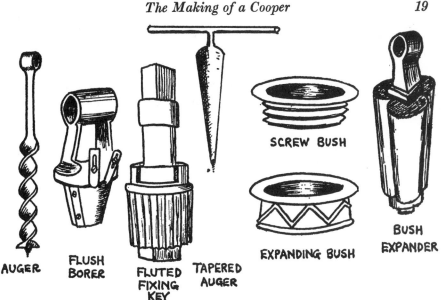

SCREW BUSH

EXPANDING BUSH

BUSH EXPANDER

AUGER

FLUSH BORER

FLUTED FIXING KEY

TAPERED AUGER

2. Tools used for inserting bushes into casks.

site the bung stave. Again the keystone cant is selected for its toughness because obviously this piece of wood must take a lot of punishment. If a cask were to leak around the bush it was always possible to take out the bung, or shive, as it was called, and tighten up the bush with the bushing tackle, which gripped the inside of the bush when turning. A type of brass bush was patented by Oldham Brothers' cooperage at Burton in the 1950s which was fitted into the cask by a tool which caused the bush to expand and bite into the wood; a stronger job, and capable of withstanding tremendous pressure. These bushes are drawn above, together with the tools used in the bushing of casks.

I seemed always to be hammering and driving, that is using a cooper's driver, which is held on to a hoop and hammered, in order to force the hoop down tight on the cask. You learn to do this quite quickly, so that almost on the instant of contact between driver and hoop the hammer strikes; you therefore start to swing the hammer before you have the driver in position, and if for some reason the driver does not make a good, square contact, then it is not possible to stop the swing of the hammer and your left hand might take some awful punishment. When my father was hammering and driving a cask I was expected to help him on the opposite side until the cask rang like a bell upon our ear-drums. You can always tell a cooper by the thickness of hard skin built up on the inside of the thumb of his left hand where he holds his driver, to say nothing of hard skin that forms on the hands of anyone who swings a hammer every day.

I was given the job of sharpening all the tools; of grinding them on a treadle wet stone which was started by pushing round with your hands, and if you caught your knee under the trough when you were treadling it caused you to hobble for a week. It was necessary to keep the stone wet and grind away until you could feel an edge on the other side of the blade. You then rubbed off this edge on an oil-stone, and honed the blade until it was capable of 'gauging out a fly's eye'. One way of testing for sharpness was to let the weight of the tool carry it through a piece of flag; if it left a ragged edge it was not sharp enough. By sharpening the tools I learned their names. I soon knew the adze, the croze and the chiv, the different types of knives, the jointer, the buzz and the downright, the various inside shaves and the swift, and I suppose I developed a pride in the efficiency of the tools by keeping them sharp, and acquired a healthy respect for them.

'If a tool falls from the bench,' my father would say, 'never try to stop it. It'll cut your fingers off.' And it certainly would. This is something you really need to learn because it is in our instinct to stop something from falling. You will have gathered that a cooper has a bench, but he never works at it; it is solely somewhere to rest his tools for convenience, unlike almost every other trade.

One day I was called from the noisy, smoky cooper's shop to tread the thickly piled carpets of the offices of the heads of the company, and in the presence of the managing director, Mr Bernard Dixon, another director, Mr John Tabor, a grandson of the founder of the company, J. W. Green, Mr Percy Lovell, a director and secretary, and Mr Cecil Holloway, who was to succeed Mr Lovell as secretary on his retirement, to sign my indentures, after being warned of the gravity of the document. It was not long before I was walking back along those 'corridors of power' requesting that my pay, as laid down in the indentures, be somehow tied to the rising cost of living, and I received a sympathetic response.

After a few years I could boast of being able to make a barrel on my own, and I will endeavour to explain here just what is involved in learning how to make a cask right from the beginning.

Every cooper knows what length of stave he needs, and how far round he wants the cask to be in order that it should hold the correct amount; so he cuts his timber, or has it cut, into the appropriate lengths, widths and thicknesses, and inspects each piece of timber to make sure it is properly quartered (see Chapter 4), and that it has no blemishes, shakes or sap. (For a summary of cask lengths and dimensions see Chapter 2.) It is possible that a blemish on the convex side of a stave might cause it to crack when being bent, while on the concave side the blemish could possibly be hollowed out and therefore would not matter. The shaping of the staves in their straight state is called *dressing* the staves. Working 'piecework', that is being paid for what you do, a cooper might dress four sets of firkin staves, or two sets of barrel staves, before breakfast, having them raised-up ready for firing immediately afterwards.

The next thing to do when you dress your staves is to list them. In fact you chop a list, which is an angle and a taper on the edges of the staves, to give them a rough shape as in the drawing below (fig. 3). To do this you have to hold the stave firmly in the left hand across the block as in the picture, and with the axe cut a rough list on the stave, working from the centre outwards to the ends of the staves, cutting off chippings. The handle of a cooper's axe is offset so that you don't chaff your fingers on the stave (fig. 4). If ever I listed the staves so that no part of the sawn edge was left showing, then my father would 'take me up on it' and regard it as being wasteful of good timber (*pl. 1*). After a great deal of practice a cooper can become very skilled with an axe. Some coopers could boast of being able to lay a silk handkerchief on their block and list a set of staves without so much as catching the silk. One Bristol cooper of the middle nineteenth century was said to be able to list staves so accurately that he did not need to use the join-

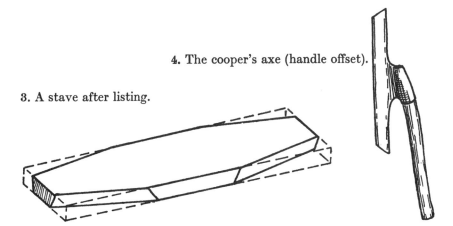

4. The cooper's axe (handle offset).

3. A stave after listing.

ter plane afterwards, but could bend the cask knowing full well that his axe-made joints would match and form watertight joints. Of course, it must be remembered that these coopers would be working with the best-quality Memel Oak, perfectly straight-grained and relatively softer than the English or American Oak. The chippings made by the axe have been the cause of much contention and even litigation. A High Court Judge was called upon to rule that a cooper's chippings were, in fact, his own property, after a cooper, working at the docks, was taken to court because he took a sack of them home for firewood. This ruling has been accepted by employers ever since, and in a booklet on pay and conditions, issued by the Coopers' Union, is an article stating, 'Chips to be allowed'.

Having listed the stave, you must now proceed to *back* it. This is the shaping of the outside, or the back, of the stave. With staves of firkin length or shorter this work is done on a horse (*pl. 2*). You sit on a horse and grip the stave in a kind of vice-lever operated by the feet, leaving the hands free. With long staves of kilderkin, barrel, hogshead or longer, this job is done on the block, holding the stave by pressing down on the end with your stomach, and keeping the stave wedged between the edge of the block and the hook, as illustrated in the next process. In backing, shavings are taken from the shaded area in the drawing below (fig. 5.).

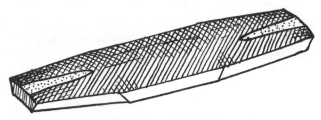

5. The stave after backing.

Here again taking too much off the stave is called *robbing* it of its stoutness. It is very easy with a good sharp backing knife, the longest of all the cooper's knives, to dig into the wood, particularly if the grain tends to run that way. I've spent many a day at the block, and on a horse, dressing staves until the shavings were almost built up to my knees. This is the easiest part of the dressing process.

The stave is now turned over and the inner side is shaped with a hollow knife as in *pl. 3*. This job is appropriately called *hollowing out*, and shavings are taken from the shaded area (fig. 6). In order not to *rob* the stave the cooper should make sure that the saw marks are visible all the way round, and that the stave is not hollowed out so much as to take away some of the stoutness in the pitch, the centre, nor at the ends.

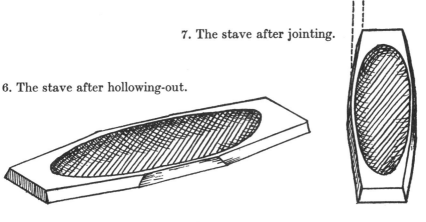

7. The stave after jointing.

6. The stave after hollowing-out.

The stave is now ready for the last and most important process in the dressing of staves, that of *jointing*, where they are pushed down what is, in effect, an upturned plane some 6 ft. in length, called a jointer. It leans against either the block or the beek iron, propped up on jointer legs to raise the top end some 18 in. above the ground. Jointing is one of the most skilful of all jobs in coopering, and the cooper is required to get just the right amount of *shot*, or angle, on the edge of the stave corresponding to the radius of the cask on the end and in the *belly* (*pl. 4*). Jointing determines the amount of belly the cask will have. The cooper calls this *height*, so that a balloon-shaped cask is said to be too high, and if a cask is made with not enough height, that is if the staves are too straight, it is said to be box-shaped. Your work might well then be referred to as being carpentry, and being a cooper you would feel somewhat insulted. It takes a vast amount of practice to acquire the accuracy necessary to make leakproof joints and to be able to hold the stave to your eye (fig. 7), and gauge the height of the cask. I first learned to use the jointer by jointing small *slight*, that is thin, bucket staves which are, of course, straight, and need only to be at an angle and tapered. To make the jointer work more easily, the cooper rubs raw linseed oil into the beech wood so that the staves slide down with less friction. I remember holding a bucket stave over at an angle and forcing it down over the upturned blade, and then, too late! The stave slipped over, trapping my hand underneath it, and down the blade it went, shaving off the nail of my forefinger, together with a sliver of flesh as far as the knuckle. I still have the scar to this day. With some tools an apprentice needs, perhaps, to learn the hard way. After the second world war metal jointers started coming into use. These were very effective for the straight joints in heads, about which I shall write later, but somehow the wear on the old beech jointers seemed to 'sympathize' with the wood in the jointing of staves for new work, and make it easier to turn the curve in the belly of the stave. These old beech jointers were reconditioned by fitting pieces of beech on to the worn patch in front of the blade, but for all new work we always kept a jointer which was nicely worn in. With that jointer I've been able to take off a shaving the whole length of a barrel stave. Talking of shavings reminds me of the time when old Sam Kilby used to send one of his men down to the local for a jug of beer. He used to write out an IOU on a jointer shaving. He must have been a very trusting sort of bloke, for he gave the job of collecting his beer to an Irishman he'd just set on. After two or three weeks he popped into the pub to settle his account and was confronted with half a sackful of shavings. 'My dear eyes!' he exclaimed in surprise, for he never swore.

After the staves have been dressed they are *raised up*. This involves putting the staves together in a raising-up hoop prior to the cask being bent. It is interesting to note that in Colonial America a 'raising' ceremony was held when the main posts of a house were erected. The size of the raising-up hoop, together with the length and height of the staves, will determine the capacity of the cask. In order to allow for shrinkage a cooper always makes his casks oversize, 6 pints allowance being made on a 36-gallon barrel, and 2 pints on a $4\frac{1}{2}$-gallon pin. You must therefore fill your raising-up hoop just right. A cooper stacks the staves against his knees, holds the raising-up hoop at the right height, and begins to fill it, holding the staves against his left knee (*pl. 5*). The staves must be matched according to toughness. If a soft stave is placed between two hard ones it will be forced outwards and crack either in the firing or later in wear. With all the necessary staves raised up in the hoop, the hoop is hammered tight. Sometimes a hoop will refuse to tighten on a cask, and every time the hoop is hammered on one side it will jump up on the other. To remedy this the cooper chalks the insides of his hoops so that they grip. No cooper would ever be without his piece of chalk. In order to tighten any hoop on to a cask it

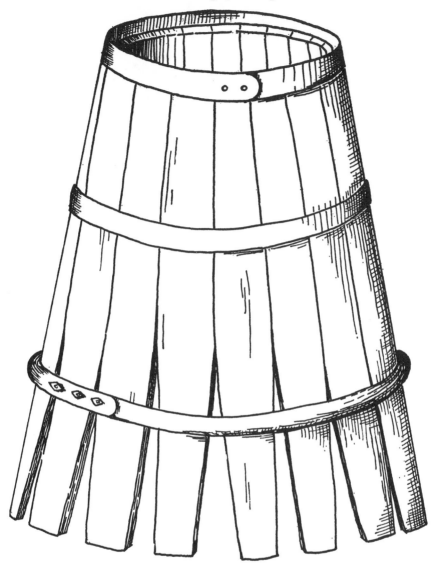

8. The raised-up cask.

must first be dry, and preferably chalked, and the cooper hammers gently at first until it is sufficiently tight for the weight of the blows to be increased. The next step is to drive the *runner*, a truss hoop made of 2 in.-thick ash which is eventually used in the firing, or bending, of the cask, down over the cask, pulling the staves together and thus giving another indication of the height of the cask, as can be seen in fig. 8. The raising-up hoop, and a booge hoop, fitting a third of the way down the cask, are now driven tight and the runner is removed. We now have the cask ready for firing. Things can go wrong in raising up a cask. If a cask is not raised up perfectly straight and upright the extent of the leaning will be much more noticeable after the cask is bent. Sobriety has not always been one of the cooper's virtues. A misshapen cask that leans to one side is called by coopers a *lord*. I should imagine that this term has the same derivation as the saying, 'Drunk as a lord', the cask being drunken. There have also been some notable radicals among coopers, from Thomas Venner, a London cooper and a Fifth Monarchy Man, who was hanged, drawn and quartered in front of Swan Alley in 1661, to Will Crooks, one of the first Independent Labour M.P.s, to whom this term might have had a deeper significance.

With a slight, that is a thin, cask, all a cooper needs to do in order to bend it into shape is to put it over a cresset until the staves are hot right through, which he assesses by holding the back of his hand against the outside of the stave, and then he starts driving his truss hoops over the cask. With a stout or an extra-stout cask, and most brewers used these thicker casks after the 1914–18 War, it is necessary to prepare the wood more thoroughly, and this is done either by steeping the cask in a tank of water which is kept boiling for half an hour, or to put it over a jet of steam and lower a bell, or large cask, over the top of it to keep the steam raging around the cask. This softens the wood and makes it more pliable for bending. While this is going on the apprentice is busy filling a cresset, a small metal basket, with shavings, and chalking the truss hoops, keeping them in order of size so that they are ready, and sure to stick. Time is against the cooper when he starts to fire the cask because as it cools it becomes more and more difficult to bend and more likely to cause staves to crack; so if a hoop is not immediately available, or if it will not stick, this can be absolutely disastrous.

When the cask is really hot and everything is ready the cry goes up, 'truss oh!' and two coopers team up, or the apprentice will team up with his master, and the firing will commence. The cask is taken out of its steam bell or tank, and put over a cresset full of shavings, which is kept blazing throughout the firing. The cresset is always lit from the top so that it burns down, holding the fire 'in' longer and therefore causing it to burn less fiercely. The apprentice must be ready to slip the runner over the cask, and then the hammering starts, as man and boy drive the hoop as quickly as they can, down to the ground. A second runner, $\frac{1}{2}$ in. smaller in diameter, is quickly driven down over the first one.

After this another truss hoop is driven tight, almost to the pitch, the belly, of the cask. This hoop must be kept tight so that it minimizes the tendency of the staves to crack outwards in the pitch while being bent. The cask now looks like that in *pl. 6*, which shows a slight (thin) cask being bent. Now the cask is turned upside down. Through the smoke will come a shout for more shavings on the fire or 'clear that hoop!' and, with a quick wipe with the back of your hand at the sweat running down into your eyes, you are hammering away again, driving away at the hoops. The fire must be kept burning, and a small hoop is dropped over the cresset within the cask in order to limit stray shavings which might char the ends. The second runner is now driven down on one side so that the angle draws the staves together sufficiently to catch a smaller truss hoop over the top. With your eyes streaming from the smoke and smarting with the sweat you are thankful to look away and grope for the next hoop, which is also driven on in a similar manner by the hammering of two heavy trussing adzes on one side in order to catch an even smaller hoop on to the cask. *Pl. 7* shows a kilderkin in the process of being fired, with smoke belching out of the top, while *pl. 8* gives, perhaps, a clearer indication of what is actually happening. If you can imagine the noise of the hammering, the creaking of the straining hoops of ash bending staves of oak, the spitting and spluttering of the fire, the smoke and the sweat, and tired muscles being forced to keep up a seemingly desperate pace, all this mingling with an occasional oath when a hoop becomes obstinate, then you have the atmosphere. The hoop-catching process is repeated three or four times until it is possible to catch on the 'dingee', a hoop identical in size to the raising-up hoop. At *pl. 9* the smoke has cleared. The apprentice can now be left in charge of the cask to make sure that the hoops in the pitch, the belly of the cask, are kept tight; otherwise the staves would crack. Coopers have a name for a cracked stave; they call it a *duck*. As in cricket it's something you'd rather avoid. I don't know whence the word is derived, but it is used widely. The apprentice must be careful to ensure that the inside of the cask does not get too hot and blister or catch fire, and he keeps the fire burning steadily. A bucket of water is always kept handy, together with a mop made out of an old haft or broom-handle with a piece of sacking wrapped round the bottom and nailed to it, just in case the cask suddenly bursts into flames. Occasionally he must turn the cask over to make sure it gets an even firing. This firing is essential so that the cask acquires *set*, that is so that, when the hoops are taken off, the staves will remain bent and not spring into a straight position as they would if the fire were allowed to go out before giving the cask at least half an hour's firing. Having been fired, the cask is, at this stage, called a 'gun'.

You get fewer ducks when you bend a cask by hand than if you do it with the help of machinery, but much depends upon the quality and toughness of the timber you are using and the exactness of your joints; a slightly rounded joint will cause a stave to crack in the pitch.

Ask any cooper to tell you what constitutes the most agreeable, the most captivating smell and he'll tell you that it is the smell of a cask immediately after it has been fired. The piping-hot oak gives off an aroma like that of a richly spiced cake being baked.

At this point I ought to write more about the ash truss-hoops. These were made specially for coopers out of carefully selected 2 in.-thick ash, bent, cleated and riveted, and capable of withstanding tremendous tensile strain. Very occasionally, if the hoops are not inspected and maintained, an old worn truss-hoop will start to give when it is being driven on to a cask, and if the cooper has not got a spare one of that particular size he's 'had it' and will have to 'pack up'. I have seen a cooper in such a predicament throw his heavy adze into the corner, take off his leather apron and storm out of the shop. We used to strengthen hoops before they wore too badly by binding them with tarred rope. To do this, you take a piece of stave about a foot long and bore three holes into it so that a rope can be passed through the holes. This can then be used as a lever to pull the rope tight round the truss-hoop. I have repaired quite a few hoops in this way, and it was surprisingly effective. There was, perhaps, a tendency for these to slip more than other hoops, and it was necessary to chalk them more thoroughly before use.

The next thing that the cooper has to do is to put a bevel on either end of the cask and make the grooves for the heads. This is called *chiming* the cask, and it is always best to do this while the cask is warm from the firing, as the wood then seems to cut more easily; as it cools it works a lot harder.

You need to get yourself a chiming hoop, that is one which will fit on the end of the cask about half an inch below the ends of the staves to allow you to cut the staves without coming into contact with the hoop; so you drive this hoop down in place of the raising-up hoop. Then you take your chiming adze, a smaller adze than the trussing one with which you hammered home your truss hoops, and one which is kept very sharp. Lean your cask against the block as in *pl. 10* and proceed to work round the cask, 'knocking off the lumps' as the coopers say. By this you cut a rough bevel on the ends of the staves. The more slope you put on the chime, that is the end of the cask, the stouter it will appear to be, a deception which would not fool a cooper.

Casks of $1\frac{1}{2}$ in. thickness are called 'extra stout', casks of $1\frac{1}{4}$ in. thickness, 'stout', and 1 in.-thick casks are called *slight*. The life of an extra stout cask used for normal brewers' work would average about thirty-five years. At J. W. Green's brewery we had some casks which were over fifty years old in the trade. They had been kept in good repair, and it is doubtful whether any of the original staves were still part of the casks, but the heads had the tell-tale brand and cooper's mark, to which I will refer later, still clearly visible.

Having knocked off the lumps, we now have to *top* the chime with a topping plane to make the top perfectly straight. The topping plane is like an ordinary wooden jack plane which has been rounded segmentally to follow the circle of the staves. Most coopers fit pieces of steel on to their topping planes because they tend to wear very quickly working on an end grain. You use a topping plane with one hand held over the mouth of the plane, and your thumb behind the iron, and hold the cask with your knees, so that it is leaning away from you (fig. 9).

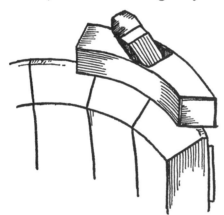

9. A topping plane.

To make sure that the top is straight you need to look across the top from two or three different directions, and 'top' a little more off where necessary.

When you're sure that the top is perfectly straight you can cut round again with your finishing adze, an adze kept extremely sharp, and make a clean job of the chime (fig. 10). It takes a great deal of practice to be

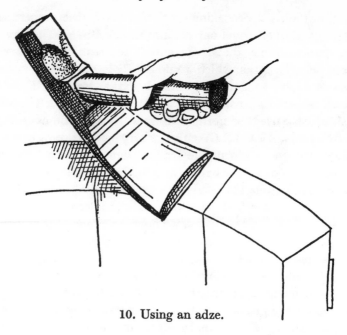

10. Using an adze.

able to swing an adze so that you cut round the chime without leaving an edge, and keep it perfectly level. I remember when I started I seemed to make a series of steps around the chime, and either the adze dug in or else I missed the wood completely. This can be pretty dangerous, and you must always remember to keep the left hand well clear and make sure that, if you miss, the adze digs into the block and not into your leg. All cooper's blocks become worn down on the side where they chime and swing their adzes, where the adze has dug into the block. During those early years of application in an endeavour to be as skilled as the master, remarks such as 'Looks as if a dog's been gnawing at that' and 'I could walk up that' were, I suppose, justified.

Where the groove is to be cut it is necessary to level the wood so as to make the circle more exact. Below the adzed chime a concave surface is produced, sometimes known as the 'howel'. This can be done with a jigger, a kind of long knife with a hollow blade and one handle (fig. 11). You lean the cask over to rest between the block and your knee, and proceed to swing the jigger with a lever motion made by swinging your right hand holding the handleless end of the tool, and cut across the grain. Many a time I've barked my knuckles on the inside of the cask as I've swung the jigger. It requires a lot of skill to use this tool, and most coopers use a chiv for this job. A chiv is a small plane hung at a fixed distance from a piece of wood which slides round the top of the cask (*pl. 11*). It cuts across the grain and therefore needs to be very keen in order to leave a clean cut. In order to get it to work more easily you must keep this lubricated with raw linseed oil on the wooden surfaces which wear. The top board is often reinforced with pieces of steel, usually of hoop iron, because it tends to wear very quickly. The varying sizes of casks make it necessary for the cooper to have a chiv for each different size, appropriately shaped. Almost all of the cooper's tools are made of beech, a fine-grained wood which wears extremely well; sometimes a piece of lignum vitae was fitted to the end that shows wear, but this was always very expensive, and more than likely strips of steel were employed in this capacity. For hafts, or stales, hickory or ash was used, preferably hickory because it is wonderfully resilient, though ash is a pretty good substitute. We used to buy pieces of well-seasoned hickory and beech for driver stocks from an old wheelwright who had his shop opposite the King Street Spire in Stuart Street, Luton. His name was Freddie Mayes, and where his shop once stood, filled with an assortment of beautifully made wheels and an old cart or two, there is now a dual carriageway taking a faster but far less graceful traffic. Every piece of wood you bought from him was carefully selected for whatever job it was to do, and individually shaped with care and skill.

To cut the groove into which the head will fit we use a croze. This is a tool with a top board similar to a chiv but with a post fitted through the board which can be moved up and down according to the distance from the chime at which the groove needs to be cut, and which is

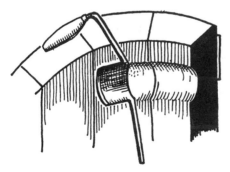

11. A jigger.

12. The teeth of the croze.

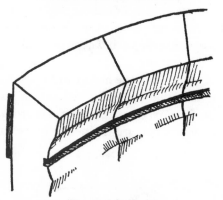

13. The finished chime.

wedged into position. On the post are fitted two teeth which cut and mark the extent of the groove, and a blade which scoops the wood out from between the teeth (fig. 12). You use this tool in the same way as you use a chiv, swinging it round the inside of the cask to cut the groove as shown in fig. 13. The croze must be kept tight against the top of the cask, otherwise you will tend to cut a rough groove, and it must be remembered that this is a very vulnerable part of the cask as far as the possibility of leakage is concerned. For making small grooves in

1. The author listing a stave

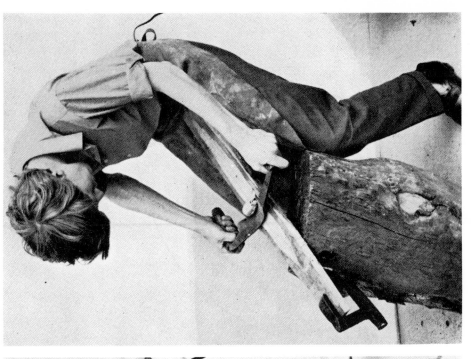

3. Hollowing-out the staves

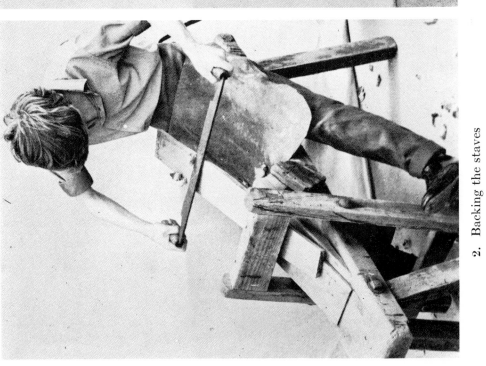

2. Backing the staves

4. The author jointing a stave

6. Firing the cask—driving down the runner

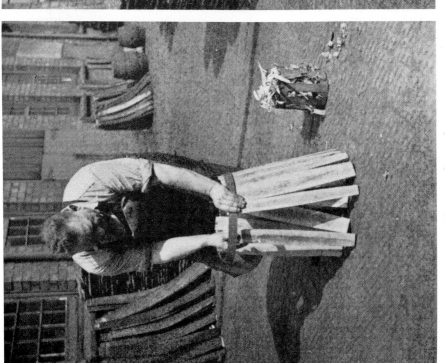

5. Raising-up the cask

7. An extra-stout cask

8. Driving on one side in order to catch-on a smaller hoop

9. Trussing adzes in unison

10. Chiming the cask—knocking-off the lumps with an adze

11. (*Above*) Chiming the cask—using a chiv to level the inside of the chime

12. (*Left*) Shaving the inside of the cask

13. Riveting the hoop

14. Boring a hole in a middle-piece of heading into which a
dowel will fit

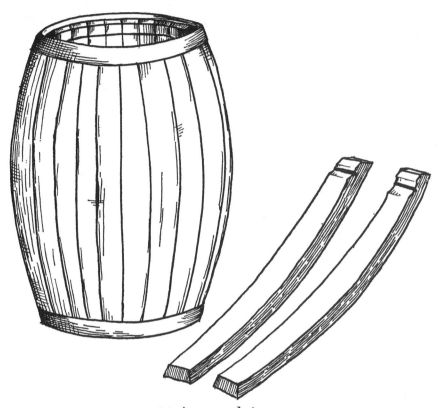

14. A case and staves.

ornamental casks a croze with saw-like teeth is used. The small cask is
held upright between your knees on a horse, and the croze is worked
backwards and forwards in a sawing motion on the side away from you.

Having cut your groove, the cask is now chimed on one end. There
was always a market for casks at this stage of manufacture. They were
called *cases*. Two old hoops were fitted in place of the working hoops,
and the case was sold to a small brewery where a cooper, working on his
own, might have been unable to fire his own casks, or for economic

reasons or perhaps because of the time element, preferred to buy cases with which to repair other casks. The cases were knocked down and the staves used in this way (fig. 14). The repairing of casks is dealt with in Chapter 2.

But to continue with the making of our cask: having chimed one end, we must turn the cask over and chime the other end. Before the cooper cuts his second groove he usually checks the cask's potential capacity with his diagonals. These are two lengths of wood or metal,

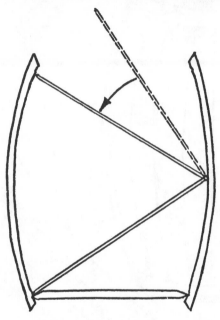

15. Diagonals testing a cask for capacity.

hinged and fitted into the cask as shown in fig. 15, from three or four different angles. By the extent to which it falls into the cask the cooper can estimate its capacity, and work accordingly, fitting the groove slightly deeper in the cask or shaving out more from the inside of the cask, so that he puts a pint or more into the cask, or takes it out, as required.

The next job is to shave the inside of the cask so that it is perfectly smooth. This is done by means of an inside shave, a small rounded plane with wooden handles on either side, or with a stoup-plane, a small rounded plane (*pl. 12*). Since these inside shaves need to follow the curve of the circle the cooper has a number of them, one for each size of cask, and shaped to the particular curve. With a small cask it is difficult to shave out the inside without grazing your arms against the inside of the chime as you shave further into the cask. The inside shaving was very important with casks used for beer; no rough patches had to be left to provide traps in which bacteria could lurk and turn the beer sour. With the constant increases in duty paid according to the strength of the beer the mild and popular beers had become progressively weaker, and because of this the danger of bacterial infection increased and made the job of shaving the inside of the cask more important. Before the first Great War, when the popular beers and stouts were brewed strong, some casks were actually *pompeyed*, that is charred inside during the firing process, in order to allow the beer to mature more effectively in the cask. Wine casks, and casks used for the maturing of spirits are deliberately blistered when they are fired, and left rough inside to allow the wine and spirit to penetrate the timber to a greater extent, thus helping it to mature.

I often used to smooth the inside of a cask, after shaving it with a stoup plane, by working a round scraper over any rough patches where the grain ran against the run of the plane. A cooper's scraper is a flat piece of hardened steel, often cut from part of a worn-out saw. One edge is ground until it leaves a sharp blade with a bevel on one side. It is then held in a vice with the sharpened blade uppermost, and by rubbing with a bar of metal, starting from the ground bevel, the cooper bends the metal blade over to the extent of about seventy to eighty degrees. This is not terribly difficult to do, and by levering the scraper against a piece of oak you can peel off a very fine shaving which will crinkle as it parts from the wood, leaving it very smooth indeed.

Before we set about making the heads to fit into the ends it is best to replace the hoops with which we have been working, with permanent ones. A hoop is always fitted together with rivets so that the right-hand side flaps over the left, and therefore keeping this in mind we take a metal hoop and fit it round the cask in order to judge where the rivets ought to be, allowing an inch or so for driving the hoop tight. We now put the hoop on the beek iron (*pl. 13*), and proceed to force cold rivets through the mild steel of the hoop and burr them over. The cooper must make sure that his rivet is central, and if he is careful and hits it with sufficient force the rivet will make its own hole through the hoop, but if it is not hit 'fair and square' it will shoot out like a bullet. While I have never experienced anyone having an accident and getting hurt in this way, many a window was shattered by a stray rivet. If a hoop needs to be made smaller the rivets are knocked through from the inside with a punch and new rivets are fitted. This the coopers refer to as 'taking up the hoop'. If a hoop is made bigger the cooper is 'letting it out'. Brewers' hoops are made of mild steel about one-tenth of an inch thick, and we always preferred to have them galvanized; otherwise they tend to rust away after about ten to fifteen years. Coopers with a vested interest in making sure that they had plenty of work might insist on ungalvanized hoops.

Every hoop on a cask has a name. The hoop that fits on the end of the cask is called a chime hoop. This is usually the widest and strongest of the hoops and takes considerable punishment when it is driven home tight with an eight-pound sledgehammer. You must make sure that you hit outwards when you hammer a chime hoop; otherwise, if it bends over inwards, you will never drive it home. A heavy maul, a long piece of steel, was a useful tool for driving the chime hoop home. With new casks the chime hoop is made so that it fits a quarter of an inch 'proud', that is above the chime, to allow for the cask to shrink, when the hoop

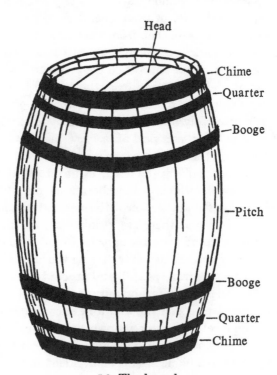

16. The barrel.

can be hammered home. In order to fit the other hoops the cooper draws a chalk line round the cask at the required distance from the chime with the help of a marking-iron, which is a piece of bent hoop iron. The cooper holds the chalk against the iron and on to the cask and, keeping the bent end on the chime, pulls it round the cask. A booge hoop fits one-third of the way down the cask, so that a booge hoop driven on both ends divides the cask into three equal parts in length measured from the bottom edges of the booge hoops. Every cask has a chime and a booge hoop on both ends. On casks of barrel size (36 gallons) or larger, quarter hoops are fitted between the chime and the booge hoops. This hoop does not have to take the same amount of tension as the others and therefore is made of much narrower metal, being held, generally speaking, by only one rivet. This part of the cask is called the quarter, and to give a cask no quarter is to give it no curve on this part of the cask so that the staves are straight from the chime to the pitch where it bends rather suddenly. Large port pipes, holding about 115 gallons are often made like this. On very large casks, sometimes on hogsheads of 54 gallons but usually on larger ones, pitch hoops are fitted much nearer the centre, that is the belly or pitch. These hoops will wear considerably with the rolling of the cask. A number of extra-stout casks made specially to withstand internal pressures greater than was normal were fitted with extra hoops for greater strength. Booge, quarter and pitch hoops were driven tight with a hammer and driver (fig. 16).

Until the beginning of this century the cooper would buy his hoop iron in straight strips and 'splay' it; that is he would make it slightly conical so that the hoop corresponded with the curvature of the cask.

For many years now hoop iron has been machine-splayed, and the cooper has only to increase or reduce the existing splay. To do this he hits the inside of the hoop, where he wants to make more splay, with the tapered side of his hammer; this is in fact what the taper on the hammer is for, and he bruises the steel, forcing it outward.

Odd pieces of hoop iron are useful for a variety of purposes. We used to cut small pieces off for wedges in the hafts, or stales, of tools, and used small pieces to reinforce the working surfaces of tools. Bits about a foot long could be bent over to be used like clothes-pegs in order to hold staves against a hoop. This is necessary when a cooper is raising-up a very large cask or vat. After an ungalvanised hoop has been on a cask for a number of years the oxide from the metal will cause a discoloration in the wood under the hoop as deep as half an inch, so that if you want to use the wood for any purpose where the appearance is a prime factor, then you need to cut deeply to remove it.

The cooper's beek iron is fitted on to a stump which is firmly embedded in the ground. The cooper's block is similarly sunk into the ground as far as it protrudes and is concreted securely. Concrete tends to wear very quickly where casks are hammered and driven, and we had our floor reinforced with metal grilles to withstand the battering.

Now we come to the making of the heads. A cooper finds the size of the head he needs by trial and error; he adjusts his compasses to roughly what he considers to be the size, puts the point of one arm into the groove and swings his compasses round to see if they fit exactly six times round the chime. He adjusts his compasses until he gets them accurate. A head might consist of any number of pieces of wood, but usually a kilderkin and a barrel would have four pieces and a firkin and pin three. The outer pieces are called cants and the inner ones are called middle pieces. These the cooper selects carefully, making sure that he has a tough piece of wood for the keystone cant into which he will bore the tap hole.

The joints in the head are made on the jointer. They are straight flush joints which are checked by putting them together and holding them up to the light to see if light shines through at any point. If it does, then it's back to the jointer until the joint is perfectly straight. We must also make sure that the joint is square, because otherwise the head will tend to lift or drop at that joint in the course of wear. The pieces of each head are fitted together by means of dowels. These are small pegs made by the cooper out of as hard an old stave as he can find. If we could lay our hands on an old length of American Red Oak this was preferable to any other, and as a boy I have sat at the block for hours making piles of dowels, chipping them roughly into shape with an adze. Machine cooperages would buy lengths of beech dowelling for this work. To bore the dowel holes the cooper uses his brace, which is an antiquated tool made of beech. The scoop-shaped, pointed bit is fixed into the brace, while at the other end a large disc of wood can be held against the chest so that pressure can be exerted downwards, leaving one hand free to hold the wood while the other turns the brace (see *pl. 14*). This has an advantage over the carpenter's brace in that, with one hand free, you do not need the help of a vice, and consequently this is time-saving.

The dowels fit tightly into the dowel holes, but before you tap the pieces of heading together you must make sure to insert a strip of flag between the joints. Choose a good thick piece and split it open with your thumb nail, running your nail down the flag.

My father always bought his flags from Metcalf Arnold, a riverman whose yard was on the Ouse at St Ives, Huntingdonshire, next to the Ferryboat Inn. He used to harvest some first-class river rushes and would call the best of them 'Coopers'. Years ago when the Elizabethans used them for floor coverings and Samuel Pepys complained of them not having been changed for twelve months, I suppose his job was of much more importance, and even until the nineteenth century, when rushes were used for mats and mattresses, but now I have no doubt that small ancillary jobs like this will finish completely.

If a cask is left empty in the sun and the wind for any length of time the joints will open as the wood shrinks. Should it then be filled, the liquor will tend to penetrate the joint, where it will immediately come into contact with the flag which will swell and seal the joint before the wood swells and 'takes up', as the coopers say.

At *pl. 15* is a picture of a head being put together.

The cooper now makes his compass-mark round the head; my father always chalked over the line so that he could see it more clearly, and then, resting the head on a saw tub, which was a firkin which had been cut down to a size convenient for sawing on, he proceeded to cut round the outside of the line, giving a wide berth on the cants, because here it is necessary to 'leave a bit on' to allow for shrinkage and squeezing of the joints. A head will squeeze as much as half an inch on the cants in the course of wear over the years; it never squeezes the other way, against the grain of the wood. To cut round the head the cooper uses a bow-saw, another rather ancient-looking tool that needs a lot of getting used to (*pl. 16*). Since the latter part of the nineteenth century most cooperages have used a band-saw driven by steam, then electricity to cut round the heads.

Next the cooper shaves the surface of the head smooth. He does this on a heading board, which is a rough board, or two pieces of boarding put together with a cross-piece of wood fixed about twelve inches from one end, and against which the head rests. The surfaces of the head are shaved smooth with a swift, a plane-like tool with wooden handles to each side. The swift can be used with and across the grain, but it is better, in order to leave a smoother finish, to work with the grain (*pl. 17*). The chalk marks are made so that the head, after being jointed, can only be assembled one way.

The next part of the job requires far more skill; that is 'cutting in the head'. This is done with a heading knife, the sharpest and most respected of all the cooper's knives, guarded and tended with the greatest of care by every cooper. Nobody borrows a cooper's heading knife. In the block you will always find two notches at right angles to each other. These were for holding the head when the body was pressed up against it, keeping it firm while the cooper proceeded to 'cut it in' (*pl. 18*). The first thing to do is to cut the top basle, which is the cooper's name for the bevel, allowing about a quarter of an inch on each cant. The top basle comes out about an inch and a half on to the head. Then the cooper marks his circle again with the compasses. Putting the head back into the block, he cuts the edge of the head to the compass mark, still making his allowance on the cants. He now has to cut the inside of the head, which has a greater depth of basle, so he uses his axe, and works round the head, taking off enough of the wood to make his work with the knife easier. With either an axe or a knife you must work with the grain; from the cants to the middle pieces. The cooper now finishes off the inside basle with his heading knife. A section through a head is drawn below.

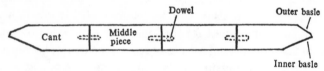

17. A cask head.

Having been 'cut in', the head is now ready to be fitted into the cask. The back head, in which there is no tap-hole, is always put in first, and in such a way that the grain is at right angles to the grain in the top head, this means that the grain of the back head runs away from the bung stave. The squeezing of the heads is therefore never acting in the same direction; they counteract each other to a certain extent. To put in a head you slacken the hoops on the one end of the cask, removing the chime hoop altogether, so that the head will be able to catch in the groove. Next we split a piece of flag and press it into the groove with our fingers before turning the cask over and tapping the head into position with the stale of the hammer. Turning the cask over, we tighten the hoops and make sure that the head, together with the flag, is nicely tucked into the groove. Any flag still showing needs to be forced into the groove with a chince, a tool shaped like a chisel with a flattened edge, rather like a shipwright's caulking iron.

Exactly how the cooper fits the second, top head into the cask, especially before any holes have been bored, has kept a lot of people guessing. It is not all that difficult, however. The hoops first need to be slackened just sufficiently so that the head can be lowered into the cask and pulled up into the groove with one hand, while with the other hand you tighten the hoop with your hammer and so hold the head firmly in the groove (*pl. 19*). In order to hold the head a cooper screws a heading vice, a tool like a large gimlet, into where the tap-hole will be bored, and pulls the head into position with this. If he did not wish to make any hole at all he could always push a piece of hoop iron through a joint between the staves and lever it up in this way. Alternatively, if you have a bung hole bored, you can insert your knocker-up through the hole so that it comes up under the head, and lever or tap the head into position from within the cask.

Now we have the cask all put together, and it only remains to smooth the outside, and this we do with a buzz, which is a scraper fitted into a wooden holder with two handles which serves to give the scraper leverage. We remove the hoops as necessary, making sure that we do not knock off too many to let the head fall out, and proceed to buzz down the cask. (*pl. 20*). If the joints are rough it is easier to precede the buzzing down by levelling the joints with a downright, a tool similar to a swift but smaller.

The last job is to hammer the hoops home, and drive them so that the cask rings like a bell (*pl. 21*). In hammering a hoop it is always wise to realise that the weakest part of the hoop is where it is riveted and, when the hoop is tight, to refrain from delivering a blow on the rivets, otherwise the hoop may break and career across the shop with a tremendous 'twang!' This can be rather soul-destroying after having put a lot of hard work into driving a hoop tight. However, all being well, and if you have learnt your lessons, the cask is now complete. The old tradesman, with his wonderfully cunning hands and keen eye, could go home proud and with a sense of satisfaction after his day's work, knowing that he had made something that would give service for perhaps half a century.

CHAPTER TWO

The Branches of Coopering

It cannot be said that at a certain time in history coopers began to specialize. The emergence of specialist branches was a natural and gradual development, as coopers tended to concentrate on work which was most profitable or least competitive, or where there were local advantages such as in a particular demand, timber or skill. The growth of trade encouraged and consolidated the specialist.

There was an acceptance among coopers that certain branches required more skill than others, and three main classes of coopering became recognized. The most skilled of these, the wet cooper, would be capable of performing any type of coopering, and some coopers did not specialize completely but undertook such varied work that they were known as general coopers. As trade contracted the search for other outlets made general coopering more prevalent, but latterly some coopers have of necessity had to specialize in spirit work, the only remaining coopering of any note.

The three main branches were wet, dry and white. The wet cooper made casks with a bulge to hold liquids. The dry cooper made casks with a bulge to hold a wide variety of dry commodities. The white cooper made straight-sided, splayed vessels. But within these branches one could differentiate between the type and the quality of the work done. The beer, wine and spirit side of wet coopering demanded much greater precision than the oil, tar and pitch side where casks of a poorer quality were used. Internal pressure resulting from fermentation was a factor to be considered by the former, as well as the greater value of their contents, but amongst these the brewers' coopers might well have claimed that their casks needed to be stronger in order to undertake repeated journeys, and to be smooth inside for easy sterilization as opposed to the wine and spirit casks which were deliberately blistered and left rough. Dry coopering differed with regard to every commodity for which the casks were used. Herring coopers, and others who in earlier years made casks for preserving fish, were called dry-tight coopers, since although their work came under the category dry, it still had to be capable of holding brine. Butter and soap cask-making was also regarded as dry-tight work. At the other end of the scale there were the apple and tobacco barrel coopers whose frail, dry-slack casks were made from the cheapest timber just sufficiently bound to last one journey. Most hardware was shipped in strong dry casks. Specialist white coopers were few, and confined to large cities and to cheese-producing areas, though village coopers through the ages were very largely employed on white work. The making of large vats was under-taken by wet and white coopers.

THE WHITE COOPER

Without doubt white coopering was the oldest branch, since the first coopered vessels of which we have evidence were buckets; it was also the first branch to be affected and to fall in the industrial revolution. Until then, wooden buckets were the commonest product of the white cooper, and they were still in use for commodities for which metal was unsuitable because of taste, chemical reaction or fire risk, until the introduction of the plastic bucket. Some racing stables still insist upon using wooden buckets, since thoroughbred horses are easily startled by the clang of metal pails, and tend to chew plastic ones, and a metal hoop is fitted around the inside of the top of the pail. The yoke and two buckets were a common sight for hundreds of years. A bucket can be defined as a single-handled vessel, and was known by such names as pail, boake, noggin and piggin in Ireland, and luggie in Scotland; a tub was a straight-sided two-handled vessel. Tubs were used for all manner of industrial processes through the ages, dyeing, building, brewing, distilling, mining, metal-work, glass-manufacturing, and in all old prints of work being done tubs are in evidence. Dolly tubs for washing clothes were in regular demand in laundries and in the home. In the cheese-producing regions in particular white coopering was in demand, but all dairywork relied upon coopered vessels; pails for milking and churns for making butter were popular since the Iron Age. The churn had a removable lid through which a hole in the middle allowed a plunger, sometimes called a podger, to be moved up and down, churning the cream into butter fat by means of a disc of wood fixed to the end. Large houses employed servant girls in special butteries. Barrel churns were also widely used. This is well illustrated by Pyne in *pls. 22 & 23*. Kitchen tubs for pickling and for flour and bread, and ornamental tubs to house that *pièce de résistance* the aspidistra, and stoups were all the province of the white cooper.

The last cooperage in London specializing to a large extent in white work, George Shaw of Poplar, established in 1882, closed down some years ago, the business being taken over by J. and W. Burman of Burton-on-Trent, established 1889, who supply flower-tubs, wash-tubs, log-buckets and pails to a very small discerning market.

To make a splay cask the white cooper would first cut his timber to size. He would then roughly shape the splay and the shot with his axe on the block, after shaving the outer, convex side, and hollowing the inner, concave side with his knives, on a horse. The staves would then need to be jointed on the jointer. With the staves then dressed he would proceed to raise them up within a hoop, and to drive the hoop tight. Although it was not essential to fire a splay vessel, a slight firing did help to knit the joints. Sufficient hoops would be driven on to the tub and it would be ready for chiming. The vessel is then rammed tightly over another tub in order to get it to the right height for comfortable working, and, leaning it against the block, the cooper adzes the chime. He then puts the tub on its side on the horse and shaves the inside in order to make the curve and smooth the joints in preparation for cutting the groove. It was held firmly in position by pressing the body against the tub so that both hands could then be used holding the bucket-shave, a tool similar to a large spokeshave, through the open ends of the tub (*pl. 25*). The groove was cut with the tub upright on the horse, using a small, saw blade croze, and working on the far dise of the tub (*pl. 26*). At fig. 18 is a drawing of a white cooper's saw-croze, with two handles fitted above the board for holding the tool as in *pl. 26*. This croze is from an old wheelwright's shop in Cambridge-

18. A white cooper's home-made saw-croze.

shire, and is in the Salaman collection. Larger tubs or vats would be done similarly on the ground, or if practicable, leaning against the block. The heads were made in the same way as cask heads, and the hoops were also made in the same way. Sometimes, for ornamental work, brass or copper was used, but with the constant tension these metals tended to become brittle and to snap in the course of time; copper- and brass-plated steel hoops were much more efficient. These were driven tight, the open end planed square with a topping plane, and a scraper used to make sure the joints were all level. The tub was then complete.

	Length (inches)	Head (inches)	Open end (inches)
BUCKETS			
House Pail	12	10	12
Stable Pail	13½	11	13
Brewers Pail	10	9½	12
Funnel	7½	13	16½
Shaw's Water Funnel	6½	12	10
Shaw's Brewery Funnel	7	14	12
Naval Buckets (Large)	12	11½	14 with lugs
(Small)	10	10	12½ with lugs
(Fire)	12¼	7¾	10½ with lugs
TUBS			
Dolly	21½	18½	21 Chime 3 in. clear of head
Naval Washing Tubs			
Large	10	18	20
Medium	9	16	18
Small	8	15	17
Naval Cooks Tub	23	31	33
Naval Yeast Tubs			
Small	22	20	25
Large	28	25	30
Naval Grog Tub	19	25	19¾
Naval Spit Kit			
Large	8	16	18
Small	6	12	41
Naval Bread Barge	20¾	17	13

Harness Casks (tubs with hinged lids, used for holding beef) of 1, 1½, 2 and 3 cwt. capacity.

Butchers' Scalding Tubs with loose heads, round and oval, 20 to 22 in. high, 30 to 42 in. diameter at top, and of 12, 18, 27, and 54 gallon capacity.

Oval wash tubs—all sizes.

Oyster Tubs, for fishmonger display,

6 in.	10½ in.	12 in.

Flower-pots were made in a multitude of sizes, legs cut from the staves and alternate staves of teak and American white elm, and with patterns cut into the top end.

Splay casks were set up in bars to these specifications:

	(*inches*)	(*inches*)	(*inches*)
8 gallons, 3 quarts,	15½	16	19
89 gallon	36½	27	32
500 gallon	92	54	74
	20	47	50
	29½	20	32½

Both ends headed
for all the above

Round Splay Storage Vats holding up to 5,500 gallons, and Oval Splay Vats were made to brewers' specifications. A common oval one was a 500 gallon with measurements:

85	50–63	39–50

Raspberry Splay Casks, sometimes called Saddle Kegs, were made in these sizes:

14	17	19
12	15	16¾
10	12	13½

THE DRY COOPER

Casks were a relatively cheap and strong means of packaging, and quite easily moved about, a tremendous advantage in times when everything was manhandled between horse and cart and boat. It is therefore understandable that there were few commodities not shipped in casks of some sort or other. The dry cooper, the least skilled if not the least proud, was responsible for making most of these casks which served such a wide variety of commodities.

The most skilled of the dry coopers were those who made the tight casks which were capable of holding liquid, the work being called dry-tight coopering. In this group were the soap, butter, syrup, gunpowder, herring and other fish-cask makers. The herring trade, at its peak in 1913, employed 1,500 coopers making casks for six

19. A harness cask.

19a. A funnel.

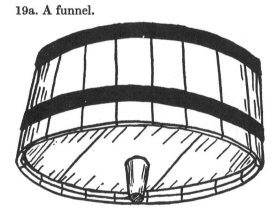

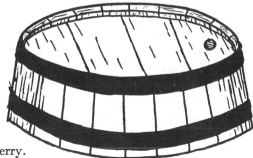

20. Saddle keg or raspberry.

months of the year, and moving with the fishing fleets during the busy season. Just before the Great War a million barrels were produced yearly, but in 1968 less than 50,000 were made in Scotland and none in England; the herring trade being practically finished. These casks were made of Swedish spruce of ¾ in. thickness, with heads of Scotch spruce or fir, and weak spots in the casks were puttied inside and tarred outside to prevent porosity. There was no backing or hollowing of the staves; they were raised-up and steamed, and in the chiming the top end, which was left with the head loose to be headed up when filled with herring, was cut round with a flincher, a type of chiv which cut a bevel almost to the groove and enabled the head to be fitted more easily. A cross-section of the end of a stave is at fig. 21. A V-shaped croze blade was sometimes used to make the groove, and the head was cut in this shape. To shave the outside of the cask a plucker was used. This is a tool the obverse of the inside shave, and did the work of the downwright. The heads were put together with nail dowels.

21. Curve on the chime made by a flincher.

Thousands of coopers worked in the docks when practically everything was transported in casks, but their numbers have gradually dwindled. The coopers working on meat casks were being made redundant with the introduction of refrigeration in the last quarter of the last century; the sugar coopers never fully recovered from the slump of the 1870s caused by the rise of the sugar-beet industry, and they went early this century; the tobacco coopers have continued up to this last decade.

15. (*Upper*) Fitting together the head

16. (*Lower*) Sawing round the head with a bow-saw

17. Shaving the head smooth with a swift on a heading board

18. Cutting-in the head

19. (*Above*) Pulling the top-head up into the groove

20. (*Left*) Buzzing down the outside of the cask to make it smooth

22. The barrel churn, as W. H. Pyne saw it in use

21. Driving the hoops

23. A collection of dairying utensils—the work of the White Cooper

24. 'Justly proud of his day's work'

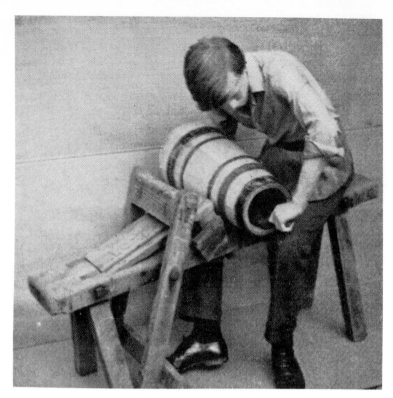

25. Using a bucket shave in making a butter churn

26. Using a bucket croze (a saw croze)

27. (*Upper*) The eighteenth-century French wine-cooper portrayed
in the process of making a cask

28. (*Lower*) The eighteenth-century French wine-cooper
completing a cask

29. A distillery cooperage

30. Bass machine cooperage, late nineteenth century

The principles involved in dry coopering are basically the same as those in any other branch of coopering, but the work differs considerably, mainly because the timber used is cheap, mostly soft and often second-hand, and the work is not so demanding as in other types of coopering, the goods held not needing such expert packaging, and the casks are made to last one journey only. The frailer casks are made from very slight $\frac{1}{2}$ in. and even $\frac{3}{8}$ in. timber, jointed, raised-up, steamed and the staves bent by pulling them together with a Dutch hand, a tool like a hand-operated windlass, where a rope is gathered round the staves and levered tight by means of a piece of wood. In this position the hoops are fitted on to the cask and the cask is put over a fire in order to give it 'set'. For the better casks metal hoops were used, of a very thin gauge, which were sometimes beaded or curved for added strength, or split hazel hoops; and for the cheaper ones split hazel, coiled $\frac{1}{4}$ in. elm, or just wire. In the very slight, that is thin, casks a groove of any depth would have weakened the staves too much; instead a hoop was sometimes nailed inside the cask, the head dropped on to this, and another hoop nailed over the top, thus securing the head.

Many of the cheaper casks were lined with paper sacks.

Machinery was adapted to the manufacture of dry casks earlier than with the better-quality wet casks. Messrs Finzels of Bristol installed a steam cooperage for making tierces, casks for provisions on board ships, in 1874. Many such firms sprang up in London. Machinery, with its inevitable waste of timber, was more economical in manufacturing casks made of cheaper timber.

The little dry cooperages that were dotted about the quaysides of every port, and prominent by the stacks of old casks that often hid the ramshackle shops, were called 'bobbing yards'.

A SELECTION OF THE TYPES AND SIZES OF
DRY CASKS

Type	Length (inches)	Diameter across head (inches)	Diameter in pitch (inches)	Timber
WHITE LEAD, COLOUR, PAINT AND SHOT WORK				
	31	21	25	old lard,
	28	19	23	paraffin,
	26	17	$20\frac{1}{2}$	claret,
	23	15	18	tobacco
	20	$14\frac{1}{2}$	$17\frac{1}{2}$	casks,
	$17\frac{1}{2}$	$11\frac{1}{2}$	14	oak, elm,
	15	10	$12\frac{1}{2}$	fir
	13	9	11	
10 quarts	$11\frac{1}{2}$	$8\frac{1}{2}$	10	
9 quarts	11	$7\frac{1}{2}$	9	
8 quarts	11	$7\frac{1}{4}$	$8\frac{1}{2}$	
7 quarts	$10\frac{1}{2}$	7	$8\frac{1}{4}$	
6 quarts	$9\frac{1}{2}$	$6\frac{1}{2}$	$7\frac{3}{4}$	
5 quarts	9	6	7	
GOVERNMENT LEAD AND EAST INDIA WORK;				
	27	17	$20\frac{1}{2}$	old lard,
	24	15	18	paraffin,
	$20\frac{1}{2}$	14	17	claret,
	$17\frac{1}{2}$	$11\frac{1}{2}$	14	tobacco
	15	$9\frac{1}{2}$	$11\frac{1}{2}$	casks, oak, elm, fir
GREASE WORK				
1 cwt.	18	$12\frac{1}{2}$	$15\frac{1}{2}$	
56 lb.	15	10	$12\frac{1}{2}$	
28 lb.	12	9	11	
14 lb.	9	$7\frac{3}{4}$	$9\frac{1}{2}$	
7 lb.	9	6	$7\frac{1}{2}$	
BUTTER TUBS				
	18	12	$14\frac{1}{2}$	
	16	$10\frac{1}{2}$	13	
	14	10	$12\frac{1}{2}$	
Jar cask	13	8	10	

Type	Length (inches)	Diameter across head (inches)	Diameter in pitch (inches)	Hoops	Timber
OYSTER BARS					
Trebles	13	10	12½	8	
Large Doubles	12	9	11¼	6	
Small Doubles	11½	8	10	6	
Pecks	10	8½	10¼	4	
Colchesters	10½	8	10	4	old
Singles	9½	7	8¾	4	beer and
Halves	9	6	7½	4	wine
Quarters	7	5	6½	4	oak
SOAP WORK					
5 cwt.	36	23	28½		
4 cwt.	34	21	26	iron	
3 cwt.	32	20	25	bound	
Barrels	30	17	21½		
Half Barrels	21	14	18		
Firkins	16	12	15	wood	oak,
Half Firkins	12	10	12½	bound	fir
Quarters					
SIZE WORK					
Patents casks	20	15	18	6 iron	
Patents casks	14	9	11½	6 iron	oak,
Patents casks	15	8¼	10¼	wood	fir
LEAD WORK					
6 cwt.	25	16	19		
5 cwt.	22½	15	18		
4 cwt.	21	14	17		
3 cwt.	19	13	16		
2 cwt.	17	11	14	iron	oak,
1½ cwt.	15	10	12½	hoops	elm,
1 cwt.	13½	9	11		fir
Irish Light	27½	19	22½		
GUT WORK	19½	13	15½	6 iron	oak
	14	9½	11½	4 iron	
PEPPER CASKS	28	16			old
	30	20			apple
					and
					grape
					barrels
EMERY WORK	21	14			
PUTTY WORK					
6 cwt.	31	21	25½		old
5 cwt.	30	20½	25		claret,
4 cwt.	27	20	24½		paraffin

Type	Length (inches)	Diameter across head (inches)	Diameter in pitch (inches)	Hoops	Timber
3 cwt.	25	19	23½		casks,
2 cwt.	21½	15½	19		oak,
1½ cwt.	19	15	18		elm,
1 cwt.	18	13½	16½		fir
BOTTLE BEER CASKS					
4 doz.	28½	19	22		
CREAM OF TARTER					old
CASKS					grape
SEED WORK					
dry kil.	23	16	19		
two bushel	22	15	17¾		
100 lb.	20	14	17		
one bushel	17	12	14		
50 lb.	16¾	11	14		
half bushel	13½	10	12¾		
Hemp 1 cwt.	24	17	20		
Split peas 2 cwt.	26	18	22		
PROVISION CASKS					
Tierce	31½	20½	25¼		
240 lb.	29	18	22¼		
224 lb.	29	17½	21½		
200 lb.	29	17	21		
124 lb.	24½	14½	18½		
120 lb.	24½	14½	18		
56 lb.	19	12½	15½		
50 lb.	18½	12	14½		
25 lb.	18	10	13		
BEEF AND TONGUE					
CASKS	30	18	22		
	26	16½	20½		
	25	16	19½		
	24	15½	19		
	20	13	16		
	15	10	12½		
	12	8	10		
POWDER WORK					
Barrels	19	15	18		
half barrels	16½	12½	15½		
48 lb.	15½	11½	14		
quarters	13½	9	11¼		
20 lb.	12¼	8½	10½		
16 lb.	11	8	10		
half quarters					

10 lb.	$10\frac{1}{2}$	$6\frac{1}{2}$	$8\frac{1}{4}$		
8 lb.					
6 lb.					
5 lb.	$8\frac{1}{4}$	$5\frac{1}{2}$	7		

Ink work in casks rising by five gallons to 45 gallon casks with 18's 12's, 9's, 6's, 3's, 2's and 1's.

MUSTARD WORK					
112 lb.	25	17	20		
100 lb.	25	16	19		
80 lb.	23	15	18		
72 lb.	21	15	18		
60 lb.	20	14	$16\frac{1}{2}$		
56 lb.	$18\frac{1}{2}$	13	$15\frac{1}{2}$		
36 lb.	$16\frac{1}{2}$	$12\frac{1}{2}$	15		
28 lb.	15	11	$13\frac{1}{4}$		
18 lb.	$13\frac{1}{2}$	10	$12\frac{1}{4}$		
12 lb.	12	9	11		
9 lb.	$10\frac{1}{2}$	$8\frac{1}{4}$	10		

THE WET COOPER

Chapter 1 describes in detail the work of the wet cooper. As other branches of coopering began to suffer from the competition created by the machine age the wet cooper continued to prosper. Tens of thousands of coopers were busy in cooperages, breweries and distilleries at the turn of the century in competition with machinery, 630 at one cooperage, Shooters, Chippingdale and Colliers, and 400 in one brewery, Bass's of Burton. Although machine-made casks became increasingly popular during the first few decades of this century, the maintenance involved with casks, which are affected both by weather and wear, was considerable, and machines could not repair casks; therefore wet coopers felt, to a degree, secure in this knowledge. However, following the second world war the shortage and increasing cost of good timber, the competition from bottle manufacturers, can manufacturers and metal casks makers, together with the drop in strength of the popular brew caused the brewery coopers to succumb; the wine and spirit coopers continue by virtue of the fact that oak possesses properties ideally suited to the maturation of strong liquor.

The repairing of casks, which kept many coopers busy during the last few decades, called for similar skills to those involved in the making of casks. The cooper had to check the capacity of any cask he intended to repair, since it would have shrunk while in use, and it might become necessary to 'put something in', that is to make the cask a few pints larger, by inserting a slightly wider stave than the broken one removed, and, if necessary, to fit a strip of timber, a narrow middle piece, in each head to correspond to the larger diameter created. This was called re-sizing a cask, and for this work the piecework cooper received good remuneration. The staves the cooper used for repairing casks came from knocked-down cases, with staves already bent and chimed on one end. After checking the capacity of the cask the cooper examined it to ascertain the extent of damage or wear. He marked these staves with chalk, marked the staves to either side of the broken staves, and then stripped the cask, which means he removed all but one chime hoop, and took out the broken staves. He then jointed the side staves next to the broken ones in order that they should make a good joint with the new ones he would be inserting (the fibres become slightly distorted and embedded into each other during the years). A new stave, checked for width, was then jointed and fitted into the cask; the hoops were then driven back on to the cask and the remaining head was removed. Both ends of the new stave were now chimed in exactly the same way as with a new cask, and the inside of the cask was shaved smooth. The reason that cases were only chimed on one end was because casks were made of slightly varying lengths, and a stave chimed on both ends would sel-dom fit exactly into another cask. The cooper had also to make sure that the stave he was inserting had sufficient height, or belly, for the cask he was repairing, as casks varied considerably in this respect. At *pl. 24* is a photograph of my father, standing in the manner of the age, beside two stacks of repaired casks, justly proud of his day's work.

Heads wore least of all, as they were sunk into each end of a cask and therefore protected, and a cooper engaged in repair work usually found that he accumulated a stack of old heads from casks which still had years of wear in them after the casks from which they came had worn to such an extent as to be irreparable. He would often fit one of these old heads into a cask with a broken head, and shave out the brand marks before re-branding it. For this job he used his quaint old round-shave. Such a head was very appropriately called 'smuggled'. In fitting a new piece of heading the same kind of work was necessary as in the making of a new head.

When a brewer sold beer he sold a particular size of cask, not a specified number of gallons, and although he would state that he did all he could to ensure that the casks held their measure he would not

22. Le chevalet—a type of horse used in Belgium.

guarantee the quantity. By the law of averages the customer won with the casks of J. W. Green's, for we tried to ensure that they held a few pints over every time they were repaired, so that a brewing vessel holding over 200 barrels seldom filled more than 195 barrels.

If a cooper were to be 'called from the block' to repair a cask that was leaking he would be prepared, if necessary, to chince (shipwrights would say caulk) flag into a joint and always to tighten the hoops. If he found a worm hole he would drive a small punch into it and peg it, making the surface smooth with his adze. Invariably a cask would 'take up' and stop leaking after the fibres had swollen up sufficiently. The most vulnerable parts of a cask were on the chime, where, if the cask were dropped, it tended to crack across the staves from the groove, or at least to leak from the groove, and the bung stave, which was apt to crack outward, as did other staves to a lesser extent, on the pitch.

On the Continent similar techniques were employed in the making of casks as in England. The axe differed in Belgium in as far as they used one with a curved blade as in fig. 23, and instead of using a horse or holding a stave in a block hook, they used *le chevalet*, a kind of horse worked by a man in a standing position (fig. 22). In order to hold the staves against a hoop when raising-up a large cask the cooper used *la pincette* (fig. 24), specially made of wood. In England any old pieces of hoop iron were bent to serve this purpose. The casks were fired over a cresset just as over here, but metal hoops were used and driven down by hammering on to a wooden block-driver held on the hoop. *La traitoire* (fig. 25), was used for forcing tight hoops over staves. In cutting the basle (bevel) of a head, a tool called *le rabot a chanfrein*

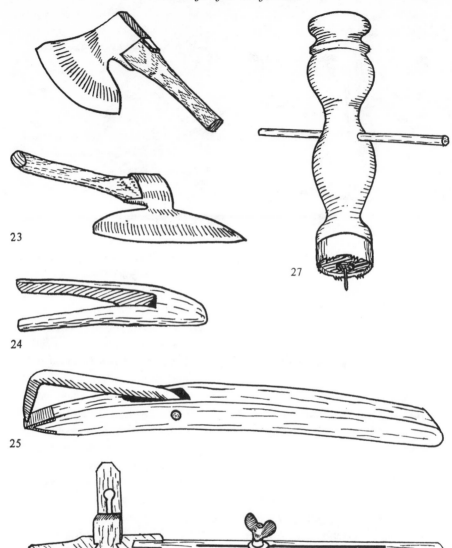

23. La doloire—Belgian cooper's axe.
24. La pinchette, used for clamping staves to hoop when raising-up.
25. La traitoire, used for forcing hoops over staves.
26. Le rabot a chanfrein, used for cutting the basle of a head.
27. Tool used in nineteenth-century France for cutting bung-holes.

was used, where a spike was driven into the centre of the head, and a plane set at an angle was worked round the edge (fig. 26). A heading knife was used in conjunction with this tool. In the nineteenth century a tool for boring holes (fig. 27) was used, a small guide hole being first bored, and then saw teeth worked round the circumference of the hole.

THE WET COOPER—WINE

At *pls. 27 & 28* French coopers are drawn making wine casks in the eighteenth century. The staves are slight, ¾ and 1 in. thick, and are being dressed in a way similar to beer-barrel staves. The horse being used is a variation of the English horse, common on the Continent and in Ireland, and is often called a shingle horse (fig. 28). Together with the horizontal jointer it is still used today (fig. 29). The knives used are identical to those in use in wine cooperages today (fig. 30). The two axes at fig. 31 were used for listing the staves, but today French wine coopers use an axe similar to the English one. The elaborate, portable block is only suitable for light wine work. In raising-up, the eighteenth-century worker appears to be involved in a seemingly unnecessary balancing act. Strange as it may seem, this is the way in which it is done today. The casks in the pictures have so little belly on them that it appears possible to bend them with a simple hand windlass (fig. 32); today a similar one on a larger scale is worked, also by hand. This would only be possible with slight timber and would be easier if the cask were heated by steam or fire. It would need to be 'set' over a fire in order that it might keep its shape, and until quite recently in some wine-growing districts coopers could be seen heating their casks over cressets in the streets. In order to chime the cask the wine cooper, instead of leaning it against the block, wedges it in a crux, or in V-shaped arms, in which the cask rests securely (fig. 33).

He used an adze which differed little from the brewer's cooper's adze, but instead of using a jigger or a chiv he used another more curved adze to cut round the inside of the cask in preparation for cutting the groove. Today wine coopers use all three tools. The chiv he calls *le stockholm*, and the adze he reserves for large casks. The croze he used was basically the same as that used today. Inside, the cask was left rough; today casks are deliberately blistered in the firing. Heads were made of a number of pieces of jointed oak, not often dowelled together. They were marked with compasses (two varieties are drawn at fig. 34), and sawn piece by piece with a bow saw (fig. 35). Similar tools are still used. The head was clamped together horizontally, and the bevel on

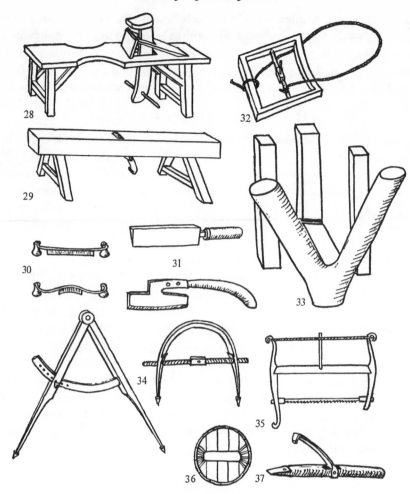

28. French wine-cooper's mare.

29. The jointer used by French wine coopers.

30. French wine-cooper's knives.

31. French wine-cooper's axes.

32. Tool used by French wine-coopers for drawing staves together in slight (thin) casks.

33. Crutch in which large wine casks were held during chiming.

34. Compasses used by French wine-coopers

35. The French wine-cooper's bow-saw.

36. The cross-piece wedged to support the (undowelled) head of a wine cask.

37. A French wine-cooper's la traitoire.

either side was cut with a heading knife. It was then fitted into the
cask piece by piece, and the head was supported by a cross piece,
wedged tightly into position as in fig. 36. Mallets and wood-block
drivers were used to force the many hoops into position. The hazel
hoops themselves were notched, flapped and bound to size. In order to
pull a tight hoop over the staves a tool called *la traitoire* (fig. 37) was
used, hooking over the hoop and pushing in the stave with a lever
motion. These casks, when rolled, would wear the pitch hoops rather
than the cask itself, and with shrinkage this hoop could be replaced by
driving all the other hoops down and fitting a hoop on the chime.
Tapered augers were used for boring the bung and tap holes, which
were also sometimes charred. Today, of course, there are many machine
shops making casks for the wine industry, but many are still being
made by hand.

THE WET COOPER—WHISKY

Whisky is kept maturing in bond for from three to ten years in casks,
namely 10-gallon octaves, 27-gallon quarters, 40-gallon American
bourbon barrels, 54-gallon hogsheads, 85- to 110-gallon puncheons and
108- to 110-gallon butts, but the vast majority are the 54-gallon hogsheads, this being the optimum size balancing maturation effectiveness,
cost and convenience. Some distilleries have almost as many as half a
million casks in bond, most of them belonging to their customers who
take them out of bond as they need them. Old sherry casks are ideal for
maturing malt whisky and they colour the spirit, although today
caramel is used. American white oak is used for making new casks in
London and Edinburgh, the techniques in manufacture being almost
identical to those of brewery casks, although the wood is slighter and
the insides are left rough. Many of these casks find their way to grain
distillers where maize is used, and the product is later blended with
malt whisky. However, the vast majority of casks used for whisky are
American ex-bourbon barrels which are sent over to England in shooks,
that is, knocked down and tied together in bundles, although some are
dispatched intact (called 'standing'), in which case they are used as 40-
gallon casks. The derivation of the word 'shook' goes back to the time
when a considerable amount of beer was sent to British troops abroad,
and as it was very expensive sending the empty casks home it became
customary to 'shook' them so that they fell apart, having first numbered the staves so that they could be put together in the same posi-
tions. In America, in order to protect the coopering industry, a law is

in force restricting the use of bourbon casks to one filling, now being changed to allow two fillings, and this is why these casks are made available to the British market. The cooperages engaged in whisky work remake these casks into 54-gallon hogsheads, the staves having to be jointed and new heads made (*pl. 29*). Techniques and the names of tools among Scottish whisky coopers differ from those of the brewery coopering described in Chapter 2. No block is used by whisky coopers; the bench is made much stronger than an ordinary bench, and the cask is leaned against it when chiming, which the Scots call, 'working out the cask'. The axe is seldom used in remaking casks. An adze is called an etch, and a jigger, a crum knife. A hollow knife is called a belly knife, and a round shave, a draw shave. To level the joints of a head, reducing the thickness of one of the pieces, the Scots cooper 'scutches' the head with his etch. Only the very middle piece of the head is called by that name; the end pieces are called cantles and other pieces are called quarter pieces. A cresset is called a lummie and a downwright, a plucker, while the beek iron is a study. A bung-flogger is used to knock to either side of the bung and force it loose; this is a long-handled, small-headed mallet. A case is called a shook or a shake.

The breweries in Scotland, when they used wooden casks, employed coopers only on repair work, all new casks being made by independent cooperages, the main ones being William Lindsay's and Neil Dryburgh's of Edinburgh, and W. P. Lowrie's of Stirling. The distilleries employ few coopers, and these are generally working on the maintenance of casks. The cooperages, therefore became large with advance contracts from the brewers. Dryburgh's made machine casks of a very high standard and in the 1930s were working a night shift supplying casks for the U.S.A. following the ending of prohibition. An export trade was also established with New Zealand, which ended some years ago. Their main machinery is now idle and, incorporated into the firm of Clark Hunter Ltd, they now employ around seventy coopers remaking bourbons.

THE WET COOPER—SAUCES AND JAMS

The famous Worcestershire sauce is matured in large hogsheads of oak, and one cooper, the last in the city, is employed in this work where the casks last for as long as seventy-three years.

In the jam industry ginger and peel is imported in casks, and American bourbon casks are used for storing preserves in the 'field'—acres of open space where casks are stacked on stillions. A certain amount of repair work, mostly cannibalization where casks are repaired from other old casks, is carried on, but there is a tendency for metal and other containers to replace the wooden casks, and no new casks are made. Some soft fruits, notably raspberries, are put into casks when picked, the flavour being unimpaired by oak, but other containers are ousting the old casks here.

TYPES AND DIMENSIONS OF CASKS, MADE BY THE WET COOPER

	Length (inches)	*Diameter across head (inches)*	*Diameter in pitch (inches)*	*Gallonage*
Butts	52	26¼	33	108
Puncheons	42	25¼	31	72
Hogsheads	37½	23	28½	54
Barrels	32	21¼	26	36
Kilderkins	26	17¼	21	18
Firkins	21	14	17¾	9
Pins	17	11¼	13½	4½
Blood Tubs	19½	13½	16½	7½
Six-gallon	18¾	11¾	15	6
Three-gallon	14¼	9¼	11¾	3
BREWERS' WORK (SLIGHT)				
Hogsheads	36½	23	28	54
Barrels	31	21	25	36
Kilderkins	25¼	17	20½	18
Firkins	20½	13½	16¼	9
Pins	16½	11	13¼	4½
BREWERS' WORK (STOUT)				
Hogsheads	37	23	28¼	54
Barrels	31½	21	25½	36
Kilderkins	25½	17	20½	18
Firkins	20½	13½	16½	9
Pins	16½	11	13½	4½
BREWERS' WORK				
500-gallon bulge vat	70	48	58 (1½ in.)	
1,000-gallon bulge vat	72	75	84 (3 in. on ends 2 in. in pitch)	
grooves 1¼ in. wide, ¾ in. deep, inside measurements:				
	62	70	80	
OVALS				
250-gallon	60	46–32	53–40½	
200-gallon	64	38–26	48–36	
159-gallon	64	31–24	40½–33½	
134-gallon	54	34–25	40½–33½	
3-gallon	17	9¾–7½		

BARRICOES In all sizes could not be made
by machinery since all joints differed; following the radius some joints needed to be almost
straight and some needed a lot of shot.

BUOYS Guinea Butts, India Butts, Common
Butts, Puncheons, Hogsheads, Barrels and
smaller.

38. THE DUTCH BOWL FLOAT (on the right)

OIL TUN 252 wine gallons or 210 imperial
gallons or 1,770 lb. Mill-pipes, hogsheads and
smaller.

TURPENTINE BARREL 2–2½ cwt.

	Length (inches)	Diameter across head (inches)	Diameter in pitch (inches)	Gallonage
VINEGAR WORK				
Hogsheads	35½	22½	28	50
Half Hogsheads	26½	19	22½	25
Quarters	22½	14½	17¾	12½
WINE CASKS				
(in gallons)				
One	14	6	8	
Two	15	7½	9½	
Three	16	8½	11	
Five	18	10½	13½	
Six	19	11½	14½	
Eight	21	13½	16½	
Nine	21½	14	17½	
Ten	22½	14	17½	
Twelve	23½	14½	18	
Fifteen	25	15	18½	
Sixteen	26	15½	19	
Eighteen	26	16½	20	
Twenty	26½	16½	20	
Twenty-two	27	17	21	

	Length (inches)	Diameter across head (inches)	Diameter in pitch (inches)	Gallonage
Twenty-four	27½	17½	21½	
Twenty-five	27½	18	22½	
Twenty-eight	30	18¼	22½	
Twenty-nine	30½	18¼	22½	
Thirty	30½	19	23	
Thirty-one	31	19	23½	
Thirty-two	31½	19	23½	
Thirty-four	32	19½	24½	
Thirty-five	32½	19½	24½	
Thirty-six	32½	20	25	
Thirty-eight	33	20	25	
Forty	33	20½	25½	
Forty-two	34	21	26	
Forty-five	34½	21½	26½	
Fifty	36	22	27½	
Fifty-four	36½	22½	28	
(sherry)				
Fifty-six	39	22½	28	
Sixty	39	23	28½	
Sixty-two	39½	23½	29	
Sixty-five	40	24	29	
Seventy	40½	24½	30	
Eighty	41	26	32½	
Ninety	42	28	34½	
One hundred	43	29	35	
(sherry butts)				
108	49½	26	35	
112	49½	26½	35	
120	54	27	36	
130	56	28½	37½	
140	57	29	37½	
150	58	29½	38½	
160	60	30	39½	
180	60	31	40	
200	60	33	42	
250	66	36	45	
300	66	40	49	
350	66	42	51	
400	66	46	55	
450	66	50	59	
500	68	55	64	
600	70	58	67	
700	72	60	69	
800	72	61	70	

		Length (inches)	Diameter across head (inches)	Diameter in pitch (inches)	Gallonage
SHERRY	Butts	50	27	36	108
	Hogsheads	39	22½	28	56
	Quarters	31	18	22	27
	Octaves	24	14½	18	13½
BOURBON	Barrels 40 gallon				
PORT	Pipes				116
	Hogsheads	39	23½	29	58
	Quarters	32	19	23½	29
	Octaves	26	15	18	14½
MADEIRA	Pipes large				
	small	50	22	28	92–96
	Hogsheads	36½	17	22	46
	Quarters	28½	13	17½	23
	13½ gallon	22¾	11½	14½	13½
	Octaves	21½	9½	13½	11½
	10½ gallon	21	9½	12½	10½
MARSALA	Pipes	49	22	28½	87
	Hogsheads	37	16	21½	44
	Quarters	28½	13	17½	22
BURGUNDY, CLARET AND WHITE WINE	Pipes	50	22	28	92
	Hogsheads	36½	17	22	46
	Quarters	28½	13	17½	23
RUM	Puncheon				90–10
	Hogsheads				45–50
HOCK	Aum				30

TONS OF BORDEAUX used to hold 900 litres, almost 200 gallons.

COGNAC was despatched in pipes of 500 and 600 litres.

WHISKY
Butts—108 to 110 gallons, Puncheons—85 to 110 gallons
Hogsheads—54 gallons, Barrels—40 gallons.
Quarters—27 gallons, Octaves—10 gallons.

		Length (inches)	Diameter across head (inches)	Diameter in pitch (inches)	Gallonage
TAR barrel					26½
SYRUP AND GINGER					
SAUCE		36	28	34	54

CHAPTER THREE

Machine Coopering

It was in 1811 that the first patent for a coopering machine was taken out by Plasket and Brown. The machine was for cutting heads. Most of the early machinery was crude and inefficient and coopers did not take these machines seriously. Before any could be installed it was necessary to fit the power unit, a steam engine, and this was an expensive proposition. When eventually power plants and machines were improved so that they became economical for large firms they called these plants steam cooperages. The first practical machines were band and circular saws, and then boring machines were introduced, and, later, planing machines, all powered by a steam engine and belts. In the 1860s large cooperages were installing steam-powered saw mills and gradually building these up into machine shops as coopering machinery was developed. The early machines, particularly the saws, were accepted quite happily by the coopers as they relieved them of heavy, less skilled work.

By the 1870s a number of cooperages were making tierces and cheap dry casks predominantly by machinery, although it was not until the late 80s and early 90s that beer, wine and spirit casks were being made by machinery in a few of the larger cooperages. At *pl. 30* is a drawing of the Bass steam cooperage of 1889; lots of men and timber with small machines spaced about the shop. By the 1890s German machine-made casks started to enter the country to compete in the market, and coopers were resentful of these developments and looked upon machinery as a serious rival.

The difficulties inherent in the development of coopering machinery were numerous. A considerable number of machines were necessary for the many different processes involved. The number of sizes of casks made it necessary to have complicated adjustable machines, or to duplicate the machines by sizes, and expensive timbers needed appropriate care and adjustment. The jointing machine needed to be made to cut the angle of shot to vary with the width of the stave, and this had to be mathematically correct to be efficient. In addition to this, inroads were being made into what was traditionally the realm of the cooper by new packaging methods and materials, and the invention of refrigeration, as well as the tendency to increasing preference among some people for bottled beers. The high capital outlay required for plant and machinery made it impossible to price the casks made any cheaper than hand-made casks; in fact they were generally dearer, and the plant needed to be worked at full capacity to be profitable, and that at a time when demand was falling. There was also the fact that all casks needed considerable maintenance, and no machine was invented capable of repairing casks.

When Messrs Larways of Bristol went over to machinery in 1904 their old rivals, E. T. Lewis and Sons, conveniently closed down. But on the other hand Shooters, Chippingdale and Colliers of London, one of the very largest cooperages, after installing machinery, suffered a financial collapse in 1913; and Samuel Kilby and Sons of Banbury were still able to compete quite successfully making casks by hand up until the 1960s. Therefore the problems which beset the interests wishing to develop coopering machinery were never completely surmounted.

Below is a brief summary of the machines used, in sequence, in the Burton Cooperage of Oldham Brothers, which was automated to a very large extent in the 1950s (the accompanying photographs are of Burman and Sons, Burton).

Staves were often first put through a surfacing, planing machine which gave them a level face side. This machine was just a horizontal table in the centre of which were revolving blades set to remove shavings.

A re-saw, a very large band saw with a four-inch-wide revolving blade, was used to cut the staves to a required thickness. A fence was adjusted at the necessary distance from the blade, and powered rollers forced the stave through. It had a feed capacity of 300 staves an hour, but the saw needed to be changed after every 500 staves.

In order to cut the staves to the required length they were fed at the rate of twenty a minute into the cross-cutting machine, consisting of two circular saws set at the stave-length distance apart. Dogs on two chains carried the timber through the saws, and the staves were then checked for shakes and general defects, before passing on to the next operation, the jointing.

The jointing machine was the most complicated of all the coopering machines (*pl. 31*). The staves were carried along a chain between two inclined and revolving knives. A template, differing according to the width of the stave and the height (amount of belly) needed for each type of cask, caused the stave to fall into the widest position between the revolving knives at the centre of the stave, thus giving the bulge. The shot, or angle of the knives, was adjusted to the radius of the head, and was reduced with wider staves. The rate of feed of this machine was eight per minute.

The hollowing and backing machine was similar to a planing machine with a revolving rounded blade set above the stave, and lowering between pre-set cams to cut the hollow, while beneath the stave, concave-shaped blades revolved to cut the rounded back of the stave. The rate of feed of this machine was five per minute with English oak and eight per minute with Persian (*pl. 32*).

Before the staves were raised-up they were laid out between two pegs on a bench to the circumference of the pitch to ensure that the cask would be the correct size. It was then raised-up over a small cylinder on a revolving stand.

For twenty minutes the casks were steamed in bells, large upturned tubs, which were dropped over a cask to trap the steam which was pouring out from jets under the cask, before being bent.

A windlass, a powered drum which pulled a steel hawser around the open end of the cask, was then used to enable the truss hoops to be caught on the end (*pl. 33*). The cask was then taken to the Buffalo machine, where it was put on a table which could be raised and lowered by the turning of a worm thread, operated by two foot pedals, while dogs on a fixed overhead frame were moved by hand to converge cn the hoops and hold them, as the cask was raised on the table (similar to *pl. 34*). Immediately the dingee, the last hoop, was fitted into place, the truss hoops were removed, and the cask was put over a fire for twenty minutes. Barrels and larger casks were bent on a hydraulic bending machine, which consisted of three inward-bent arms on which dogs were fitted that caught on to the hoops. Three electrically driven water pumps caused the arms to rise and descend while the cask remained stationary.

The cask was then taken to the croze and chiming machine, which worked on the principle of a lathe. The cask revolved at about 500 revolutions a minute while the stationary knives at each end cut the chime and the groove (*pl. 35*).

Staves of $1\frac{3}{4}$ in. and thicker could be bent singly. The cask was raised-up and steamed before being 'knocked down', that is taken apart, so that each stave was bent singly by machine pressure being exerted in the centre. This was a very slow method, but staves were seldom cracked.

The planing machine was used to cut the joints in the head.

The pieces of heading were then put into the dowelling machine, where drills of ⅜ in. diameter bored two holes, at a fixed distance apart, for the machine-made dowels to fit into. The head was then fitted together with flag in every joint.

It was then put through a thicknessing machine, which was, in effect, a large planing machine with long 30 in. revolving blades and powered rollers to force the head through the knives. At the required thickness the head would pass through the machine without touching the knives.

It was then marked out with compasses to the necessary size and put through a band saw with a blade of 1½ in. width. This blade was capable of sawing 3 in. thick timber.

To cut the basle, the head was clamped firm between two sets of revolving blades set on a V shape (*pl. 36*). The blades cut the head from the cants to the middle-pieces, moving round the head to avoid cutting against the grain, as far as two cams would allow, to cut slightly elliptically to give extra width on the cants, and elsewhere cutting in to the diameter of the head.

It was then branded on a gas-heated brand table, where the head was clamped and pressed down on to the brand irons.

Meanwhile the cask itself was being shaved on the inside on a similar machine to the croze and chiming machine. The cask was rotated, and a rounded plane, fitted on an arm within the cask, moved on to the wood, to plane it smooth. The cask revolved at 300 revolutions a minute.

After the cask was headed up (by hand) it was put on a similar machine where the cask was rotated at 200 revolutions per minute, and a plane was worked against the outside.

Hoops were riveted in a machine which punched through the iron, and burred over the rivets on the principle of the electric hammer.

Lastly the bushes were fitted into the casks on a machine which drilled the holes and inserted the bushes. And so we had the machine-made cask.

At *pl. 37* is the cooperage of J. & W. Burman, Burton on Trent.

CHAPTER FOUR

Timber used in the Coopering Trade

Casks have been made out of all kinds of timber. The earliest casks were made of palm tree wood; later the Celts used Pyrenean silver fir, and no doubt every kind of timber has been experimented with at various times, until the most suitable ones, dependent upon availability, quality and competitive costs, became the prerogative of particular branches of the trade.

In most branches of dry coopering a premium was set upon cheapness. The quality of the timber was of secondary importance. A wide variety of soft woods, firs and pines, and bastard woods were used. Article 12 of the Admiralty Book of Cooperage Instructions, issued over one hundred years ago, runs,

. . . the Master Cooper is to take great care that both new scantling and old staves are manufactured into the casks for which they will best answer, so as to be worked up to the greatest possible advantage; that the old staves which may be in his charge are to be worked up into casks, in preference to using new timber . . . and that he is never to convert new staves into scantling for dry casks when he may have old staves which can possibly be applied there to. . . .

Herring barrel coopers, the tight-dry branch of coopering, used Swedish spruce which, prior to the 1939–45 War cost £22 a standard, sufficient to make between 195 and 200 barrels, and within twenty years had risen to £140 a standard. Scotch spruce and fir were used for the heads. American white elm was widely used early in the century, but second-hand timber, from old casks, re-made into smaller dry casks, was most common.

The white cooper worked largely with oak, particularly with regard to the dairying side of the business, but beech was also used quite extensively, and chestnut, ash, elm, teak, sycamore, pines and firs and even yew were used where taste was not the main consideration

Imported hardwoods were used for ornamental work where appearance mattered.

The wet cooper needed to be very discriminating in his choice of timber. It was essential that the timber he used possessed a number of properties. Firstly it had to have a neutrality of taste, or 'nose', so that it would not impart an obnoxious flavour to any contents. In the second place it was required to have a capacity for hard wearing. It had to be capable of bending, when heated, without cracking. Fourthly it needed to have a grain so tight as to be impervious to liquid, and lastly it was necessary for the timber to have pores which would allow beer, wine or spirit to breathe and therefore to mature. Oak is the only timber which possesses these qualities, but the oak differs considerably, depending upon the climatic conditions in which it grows.

Let us first consider the principal botanical features of the oak, as shown in the diagram below.

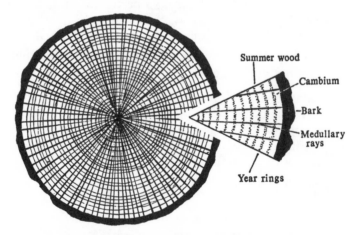

Summer wood

Cambium

Bark

Medullary rays

Year rings

39. Section through an oak tree.

The year rings are formed by the rising sap in the spring, and are very porous, while the denser wood between the rings is the summer growth. The medullary rays are relatively impervious bands of cells in the oak, which extend radially from the pith to the bark. It is when the wood is cut so as to expose these rays at the surface that the beautiful figuring effect is produced, called by coopers the flower, for which the oak is famed. This can be seen to advantage in the cocktail cabinet made from an oval barricoe, the type of cask used in lifeboats which could not roll with the rocking of the boat (*pl. 38*). These fine sheets tend to retain their shape during the seasoning, that is the drying, of the oak, and the wood nearer the heart, which has been under some pressure within the confines of the tree, has a tendency to shrink less than the newer wood in the outer part of the trunk. A piece of oak cut as in fig. 40 therefore tends to warp. It is called board oak. The piece of oak in fig. 41 has been cut on the quarter, and resists the tendency to warp. The wood between the rays will also tend to shrink and compress, whereas the rays are capable of withstanding considerable longitudinal pressure, and will not shrink. It can therefore be seen that timber for casks needs to be specially cut on the quarter.

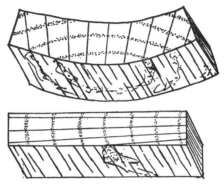

40. (*Upper*) Section through a stave improperly cut.
41. (*Lower*) Section through a stave cut on the quarter.

Until the time of Elizabeth I there was probably sufficient English oak to satisfy the needs of the coopering trade, but the competing needs of the iron-smelters and the ship-builders caused such a depletion in the number of oak trees growing in the forests of the south that great concern was felt, and various laws were introduced intended to alleviate the situation. In 1543 and again in 1585 there was legislation prohibiting the export of casks larger than barrels, and making exporters import a corresponding amount of clapboard, or thinly cut timber for casks. The Elizabethans imported quartered oak from the Hansa region of Denmark and the Baltic, and a great deal of this was used in their renowned panelling, which they called wainscot, though they did not appreciate the aesthetic beauty of the figuring, preferring to paint their panels—a sacrilege!

Pl. 39 shows an English oak. Our trees generally grow in isolation or in small woods, twisting and turning and branching off near the ground, causing knots in the timber. They mature slowly over two hundred years, thus giving a greater number of porous annual rings than in the faster-maturing trees. English oak is also a very tough wood and tends to blunt the best tempered steel after a little while. For these reasons imported oaks have been preferred. In the books of a Master Cooper of Bristol, written about 1750, staves from Hamburg and also from Virginia are included in the inventory. Up to the 1939–45 War brewers' casks in this country were mostly made of Memel Oak imported from Russia, an oak possessing a fine balance of the qualities required, having an ideal texture, being low in resinous content and therefore giving no smell.

Memel Oak takes its name from the old port of Memel on the Baltic whence the shipments to this country were first made. It grew bordering the many rivers flowing down into the Baltic Sea in the protection of forests of which oaks numbered no more than ten per cent. The wood is similar to the Danish and German oak imported by the Elizabethans. Oak is a relatively slow grower by comparison to the soft evergreen firs, and is therefore drawn upwards during the short summer growing season when the sap rises, and the plant fights for life, light and air. This causes it to grow with few branches, which cause knots in timber, and without any twisting of the grain. The top of the tree, which is called the crown, runs higher and higher, and the forester cuts away the 'nurse', soft wood trees when the oak is sufficiently tall to enable the crown to bush out, and so nourish the trunk, as year after year the cambium is converted into wood.

The Russian peasants would go into the forests in the winter when they were unable to follow their usual occupations and fell the trees while the sap was down. After felling, the bark was removed and the trunk cut into suitable lengths. It was now ready to be converted into staves, and here the skill of the woodsman came into play. He worked in a clearing in the forest with only a few simple tools. The first thing he did was to split, or cleft as it was called, the log in half, right through the heart. A wide log was split with wedges, but logs of under two feet six inches in diameter were cleft with three or four blows, delivered with a two-handed axe. The two halves were then inspected to ascertain how they could best be made into staves with the least amount of waste. The heart was never exactly in the centre, and therefore staves of varying widths were cut from each log. Each half log was then split into what were called billets, with a number of chops, radially (fig. 42).

The woodsman then marked his timber with a bow-string tied to either end of a shoot of ash about six feet long. The string was rendered

42. Section through an oak tree showing the quartered staves and waste.

with a piece of charred oak; the bow was laid along the billet, pulled sharply upward and released so as to make a black line, easily observable on the light-coloured surface of the stave. The woodsman then worked to this line with a two-handed axe.

Neatly marked, the billets were cut into staves by resting them against a log and removing the immature growth, called the cambium, near to where the bark grew. The pith and unsound wood on the opposite edge was also removed, parallel to the first edge. The billet was then turned over on to its side and the angle hewn off, leaving the stave shaped in section like a parallelogram. The stave was then finished off on a large plane worked by two men, the one pushing and the other pulling, although such was the skill of the woodsmen that little planing, generally speaking, needed to be done.

Care needed to be taken to avoid letting the staves dry too quickly in the wind, so it was customary to pile the staves, and shield them with branches. They remained in the clearings for some months until the ground was in a fit state for transporting them to the railhead and hence to the port of shipment, where they were graded and 'bracked' for quality. Before the days of the railways the staves were made up into huge rafts and floated down the nearest river to the port of shipment.

Experienced men called Sworn Brackers sorted the staves into 'best quality staves', designated and marked appropriately with a 'Crown', and second best quality staves called 'Brack'. To Brack is literally to plough. At one time the staves which were not up to Crown Standard were 'ploughed' with a scribing tool in the same way that customs officers mark the gauges and contents on spirit casks. The staves were then sorted into nine different lengths, each of which had eight graded variations of width and thickness. The longest stave was a pipe of 66 in. upward, and the shortest, 'Short short heading', cut from 17 to 19 in. in length. There were also Brandy, Long and Short Hogshead, Long and Short Barrel and Long and Short Heading.

The width of the Memel stave was twice its thickness.

At 3 in. thickness, 6 in. width, it was called a Full-Size Stave.

At $2\frac{1}{2}$ in. thickness, 5 in. width, it was called a Ten-Quarter Stave.

At $2\frac{1}{4}$ in. thickness, $4\frac{1}{2}$ in. width, it was called a Nine-Quarter Stave.

At 2 in. thickness, 4 in. width, it was called an Eight-Quarter Stave.

At $1\frac{3}{4}$ in. thickness, $3\frac{1}{2}$ in. width, it was called a Seven-Quarter Stave.

At $1\frac{1}{2}$ in. thickness, 3 in. width, it was called a Six-Quarter Stave.

At $1\frac{1}{4}$ in. thickness, 3 in. width, it was called a Five-Quarter Stave.

At 1 in. thickness, 3 in. width, it was called a Four-Quarter Stave.

Thus there were seventy-two different sizes of Memel specification.

Staves were sold by the mille of 1,200 pieces. (It can be recalled that it was a characteristic of Danelaw that it counted in sixes rather than in fives, resulting in a 'long hundred' of 120.) This was convenient in that there were 1,200 pence in £5.

In addition to these specifications there were also staves called Single Imported Staves. These were of $1\frac{1}{2}$ in. thickness and of varying widths, the price being calculated on the average width in a mille.

Until the 1920s Memel staves called 'doublet' were imported. These were cut so that at each end they were $\frac{1}{4}$ in. stouter, thicker, than in the centre. This enabled the staves to bend more easily and left the thickness in the end to give added strength where the depth of the groove weakens the casks structurally. However the pitch (centre of the cask) is left weaker and this is subject to the most wear and vulnerable to damage, and the thickness of the chime tended to deceive.

It was reckoned that in the conversion of logs into quartered staves 25 cubic feet of staves could be cut from 100 cubic feet of oak, whence the high cost, but the Crown Memel Oak Stave was as near perfect as any oak. After 1934 Memel became unobtainable in England, and Polish oak was imported which, though an excellent oak, lacked the perfection of Memel. This was imported in single staves and was more expensive.

From America we have red and white oaks, grown in the United States and Eastern Canada. They are both straight and close-grained, dense, tough and hard-wearing, but it is difficult to eradicate the acid-tasting tannin in the wood, and so these oaks tend to cause any beer to taste with a tang. To overcome this many brewers used to line these casks with a kind of pitch or rubber solution, and later with a plastic, non-toxic preparation that would resist steam sterilization. One very very large firm of brewers, noted for their stout, used to insist on their casks being made of American red oak, with the inside pompeyed, that is charred and blistered in the firing, or bending, process. This was said to help give the stout its tempting distinctive flavour. American white oak is used extensively for whisky casks, a vast number of wine and other spirit casks. For maturing whisky high prices are paid for casks previously used for sherry, as these are considered to be the best casks for this purpose. They not only help in the maturing but also impart a colour to the spirit. In the past lawsuits were brought against distillers who coloured whisky by artificial means.

It was during the wars which disrupted trade with the Continent, putting a temporary stop to the importation of Memel oak, that other oaks were, of necessity, brought into use. English oak was used quite extensively during the Great Wars, and American oak was also used. In the 1950s, with Memel oak still unobtainable at a reasonable price, Persian oak came on the market. During the immediate post-war years and until 1956, when these shipments stopped, 90 per cent. of all casks made for brewers were made with Persian oak. This oak grows in the hill forests of Persia where the climate is suitable, and after being converted into staves, much in the Russian manner, is transported down to the plains, and then for 2,000 miles travels by road in intense heat, where the timber blisters and suffers shakes (internal cracking of a honeycomb nature). Shipments varied considerably in quality, and co-operages worked with the anticipation of 25 per cent. waste. A limited amount of Polish and Yugoslavian oak was imported just after the war, but this soon stopped.

The French wine cooper uses oaks grown in the wine-growing districts, each being regarded as giving a different 'nose', or taste, to the wine. It is an age-old tradition that the trees should grow in the same soil as the grapes. South Africa imports French oak grown in the wine-growing districts in order to make casks in which to mature brandy.

Oaks grown in latitudes above fifty degrees are not regarded as being suitable for wine, although Memel oak has been used successfully for shipping port wine.

Spanish chestnut is commonly used for shipping inferior wines, and particularly for casks making only one journey. Chestnut has not the qualities of oak, but is just adequate, and very much cheaper.

THE SEASONING OF TIMBER

. . . That where grete deceit and untrowthe dayly been used within this citee, by the means of makyng of barells, kilderkyns, firkyns and other vessells wheren licor shalbe put, of sappy and grene tymber, for lacke of serche and correccion theruppon to be hadde and done, the which vessells so made, after they have been any while occupied, of necessite must shrynke, wherethrugh the same vessells at the laste weryng of theym, lacke of their true and juste measure, that they ought conteyne, that is to say, somme of them iiij galons, somme iij galons, somme ij galons, somme more somme less. . . .

So runs an ordinance put before the Lord Mayor of London by the Coopers Company in 1488, emphasizing the need for adequate seasoning and the consequences of using wet or green timber.

When demand exceeds supply there is always the temptation to use wood of this nature; it is soft and easy to work with, even though it tends to make the shop damp and the tools rust, but the trouble follows in the shrinking and, if improperly cut, warping.

It is necessary to separate planks with small pieces of wood in order to allow the air to circulate freely through them, and to leave them for between one and five years to weather. The ends are often painted to resist the tendency to crack when drying.

In this machine age man has naturally attempted to better the work of nature and to speed up the process, and timber has been dried by heating in kilns. Most imported hardwoods are kiln-dried, and have been since the war, but early attempts to kiln-dry resulted in the wood becoming 'carrotty' and brittle, and of little use to the cooper, and while this has, no doubt, been rectified, a prejudice remained amongst coopers.

THE PICKLING OF CASKS

In order to prepare the cask to hold beer, wines or spirits for the first time it was customary to fill it with a solution of brine and sodium carbonate in order to neutralize the acid-tasting tannin in the wood. The cask was allowed to soak for three days and then filled with clear water for a day before it was washed out and racked with beer. Some kinds of oak were more acid than others, and in some this pickling was not satisfactory and they were lined, but English and Memel oaks would always be sweet after pickling. Some cooperages steeped their timber in large tanks of sodium carbonate solution before they started to use it.

All casks on a brewery were smelt by a 'snifter' before being racked with beer to make sure that they had a sweet 'nose'. There was a danger of the cask becoming sour and causing any beer it subsequently contained to turn sour as well. A sour cask would be neutralized by a similar solution to that used in pickling a cask. If a cask were to be left unpegged after it had been emptied for any length of time there was always a danger that flies would get into the cask and lay their eggs among the spent hops and yeast residue. This would cause the cask to smell horribly; it would be labelled 'stinker', and the only way to cure such a cask which had become impregnated by this smell was to shave off at least $\frac{1}{8}$ in. from all over the inside of the cask (quite a job!); and if the cask happened to be worn it was regarded as a 'write-off'.

CHAPTER FIVE

Tools

Thousands of years before foundries could turn out a 'standard' model, or before textbooks were invented to describe them, the cooper's tools were the means whereby man was able to shape and make the barrels and wooden vessels which played such a large part in his day-to-day living. Prior to the last century they were often made individually to a cooper's requirements, largely based on ideas circulated by word of mouth, and consequently they varied from district to district. Specific variations and adaptations would also be made to allow for specialist work in a particular branch of the trade. The names of these tools, therefore, differ somewhat up and down the country. In view of these facts I intend, therefore, to give below a brief summary of basic hand tools in common usage through the centuries.

1 AXE: distinguished by its ten- to eleven-inch blade designed for very precise and exacting work, it has an offset haft so that the knuckles are not chaffed by contact with the stave being cut.

2 ADZE (TRUSSING): a heavy and blunt tool used for hammering home truss hoops when bending a cask.

3 ADZE (ROUNDING): a very sharp tool used for cutting the slope on the chime of the cask.

4 ADZE (TRIMMING): used in dry coopering for cutting off any protruding pieces of hoop.

5 ADZE (CHEQUERED): another dry-work tool with a dual purpose; that of trimming and removing nails with the V-shaped centre, hooking under the nail and the tool being used as a lever (fig. 43).

6 AUGER: a woodworking bit fixed to a handle, needed in two sizes for the tap and bung holes.

7 AUGER (TAPERED): again in two sizes and used in either a clockwise or an anti-clockwise manner until the hole is sufficiently large.

8 BEEK IRON (or BICK IRON): a type of anvil having one $\frac{3}{4}$ in. and one $\frac{1}{2}$ in. hole, and upon which the hoops are riveted and splayed.

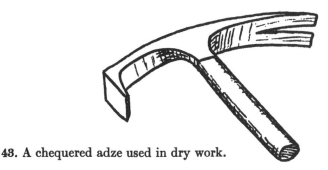

43. A chequered adze used in dry work.

9 BILGE HOOP: a hoop that is fitted on or very near the pitch, or belly, of the cask.

10 BLOCK: upon which the cooper works. It is cemented firmly into the ground.

11 BLOCK HOOK: a hook driven into the block so that a stave can be held between the block and the hook as in a vice.

12 BOOGE HOOP: drives into position one third of the way down the cask on the part of the cask sometimes called the booge.

13 BORER (FLUSH): for cutting a taper and surround for the bush to be inserted and countersunk.

14 BRACE (sometimes called a DOWELLING STOCK AND BIT): held between the chest and the wood with a fixed scoop-like bit. Has the advantage of being able to be used with one hand free to hold the wood being bored.

15 BRANDING IRON: of wrought iron with figures or letters cut almost an inch into the iron and having a long, three-foot handle.

16 BUCKET SHAVE: used in white work for shaving the inside of buckets across the grain.

17 BUNG FLOGGER: long-handled mallet type of tool used for knocking to either side of a bung in a wine or spirit cask in order to loosen the bung.

18 BUZZ: a scraper blade wedged between two handles in order to give it additional purchase against the timber.

19 CHALK: rubbed on the inside of hoops to make them stick or grip.

20 CHIME HOOP: the hoop which is fitted on the end, or chime, of the cask.

21 CHIMING HOOP: a hoop which is driven on to the chime, leaving the wood proud for chiming, that is cutting the chime into shape.

22 CHINCE: used for caulking, forcing the flag, or rush, into the joints.

23 CHISEL: cold chisel used for cutting hoop iron.

24 CHIV: the tool that levels the inside of the chime ready for cutting the groove. Different sizes are used for different-sized casks.

25 CROZE: the tool which cuts the groove for the head; one size used for barrels and kilderkins and one for pins and firkins.

26 CROZE (SAW): a small croze which cuts like a saw. Used for buckets and very small ornamental casks.

27 COMPASSES: in various sizes for marking and determining the size of the heads.

28 CRESSET: a metal-banded brazier which holds the fire of shavings when trussing the cask.

29 DEVIL'S TAIL: Scottish coopers' name for a Knocker-up.

30 DIAGONALS: two lengths of wood or metal hinged together which, when opened up inside a cask, give an indication of the capacity of the cask. Different sizes for each size of cask.

31 DINGEE: the last hoop to fit on the chime of a cask when trussing.

32 DIP STICK: a calibrated rule for dipping into a cask in order to ascertain the amount of liquor in the cask.

33 DIVIDERS: compasses.

34 DOWELLING BIT: scoop-like bit used in a wooden brace.

35 DOWNRIGHT: used for shaving the outside of a cask; cuts like a plane with handles to either side.

36 DRAWSHAVE: Scottish coopers' name for Round Shave.

37 DRIVER: the tool which is held on to a hoop (other than the chime) and struck with a hammer in order to force the hoop into position. The stock is of beech.

38 DRIVER (METAL): solid steel, used in dry work.

39 DUTCH HAND: used in dry work to lever the staves together when bending the cask (fig. 44)

40 ERASING IRON (or ROUND SHAVE): used for removing brand marks on a head, smuggling, and sometimes used for levelling joints inside a cask.

41 ETCH: Scottish coopers' name for an Adze.

42 FENDER: small hoop used round a cresset to limit stray burning shavings and so protect the cask from fire.

43 FILE: common woodworking file used for ornamental work.

44 FILE (RAT TAIL): pencil-shaped file for cutting patterns in ornamental work.

45 FLAG: river rush, harvested and put between joints to seal.

31. The jointing machine

32. The hollowing and backing machine

33. The bending machine, a windlass

34. The buffalo for driving hoops

35. The chiming machine

36. The machine used for cutting-in the head

37. A mid-twentieth century machine cooperage

38. A cocktail cabinet showing the 'flower' of the quartered oak

39. An English oak

40. The horse and block into which is fitted a block hook

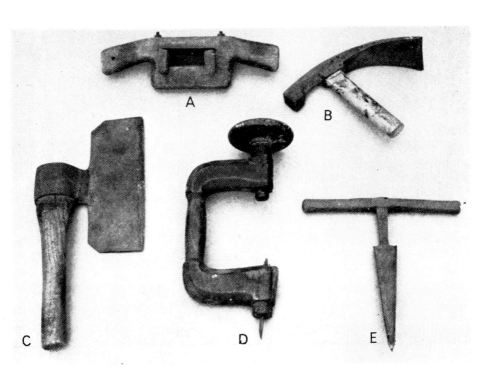

41. The buzz (A), the adze (B), the axe (C), the brace (D) and
the tapered auger (E)

42. The trussing adze (A), the bucket shave (B), the white
cooper's round shave (C), the rat-tail file (D), ordinary
file (E) rasp (F), rivet mould (G), saw chiv (H)

43. Jointer (A) and beek iron (B)

44. Jointer used by a travelling cooper in the nineteenth century. It can be taken apart for easy transport

44. The Dutch hand used for drawing together slight staves in dry work.

45. A flincher, used in herring work.

46 FLAGGING IRON: used to force joints apart so that flag can be inserted.

47 FLINCHER: Chiv-like tool with a fixed blade which cuts a deep slope on the top end chime of a herring barrel so that the head will fit more easily (fig. 45).

48 FLUTED FIXING KEY: for gripping inside a brass bush and screwing it into a cask.

49 HAMMER: generally 3 lbs. in weight and tapered on one end which is used for bruising the splay on hoops.

50 HEADING BOARD: with a piece of wood protruding for the head to rest against when it is being swifted over.

51 HEADING VICE: screws into the head to enable it to be lifted up into the groove.

52 HORSE: wooden clamp worked with feet while in sitting position, hands free to use tools.

53 INSIDE SHAVE: founded to fit inside a cask, different sizes for different-sized casks, handles to either side to shave and level the joints.

54 JIGGER: for smoothing, cross-shave, the inside of the chime in preparation for the groove to be cut, held with handle in left hand and swung with the right.

55 JOINTER: six feet long upturned plane down which the stave is pushed, the jointer having two legs holding one end 18 in. from the floor.

56 KNIFE (BACKING or DRAW): the longest of the cooper's knives, used for making the convex curve on the stave for the outside of the cask and for levelling the joints.

57 KNIFE (BELLY): term used by Scottish coopers for Hollow Knife.

58 KNIFE (CRUM): Scottish coopers' name for Jigger.

59 KNIFE (HEADING): the keenest of the cooper's knives, used for cutting the basle on the head.

60 KNIFE (HOLLOW): used for cutting the concave side, the inside of the stave before it is bent.

61 KNOCKER-UP: a bent piece of piping that is pushed through the bung hole and levers the head up into position in the groove.

62 LUMMIE: term used in Scotland for Cresset.

63 MAUL: Length of heavy steel with a handle at one end, used for hammering and tightening a chime hoop (fig. 46).

46. The maul.

64 MOP: made with an old piece of broom-handle and a piece of sacking and kept in water ready should a cask catch fire during trussing.

65 MOULD (RIVET): used for ornamental work only when the rivet needs to be rounded neatly when finished.

66 OIL-STONE: piece of natural or manufactured stone which is kept oiled and on which a tool is sharpened.

67 PLANE (TOPPING): a curved plane used for levelling the chime at the end.

68 PLUCKER: a tool used in Scotland for shaving the joints on the outside of the cask (fig. 47).

47. The plucker.

69 PUNCH (RIVET): a cooper usually has two sizes for making holes in hoop iron in preparation for the rivet.

70 QUARTER HOOP: the hoop which fits on the cask between the chime and the booge. This part is called the quarter.

71 RAISING-UP HOOP: used when putting staves together as a cask.

72 RASP: common woodworking type used for ornamental work.

73 RIVET: in various sizes for joining hoop iron to form hoops.

74 ROUND SHAVE: see Erasing Iron.

75 ROUND SHAVE (WHITE WORK): for shaving inside very small casks.

76 RUNNER: an ash truss hoop, the first that is driven over a cask when it is bent.

77 SAW (HAND): common woodworking saw used for sawing lengths of heading and for sawing staves into lengths.

78 SAW (BOW or FRAME): saw with ½ in.-wide blade used for sawing round heads before cutting them to fit the cask.

79 SCRAPER: flat piece of metal, often an old piece of saw, sharpened and bent over on the keen edge for smoothing the cask by removing fine shavings.

80 SLEDGE HAMMER: 7–8 lb. hammer used for driving home hoops on large casks or vats.

81 STOUP PLANE: small rounded plane used for shaving the inside of a cask.

82 STUDY: Scottish coopers' name for a Beek Iron.

83 SWIFT: a plane-like tool with handles to either side, used for shaving the surfaces of heads.

84 TOPPING PLANE: see Planes.

85 TRUSS HOOP: an ash hoop some 2 in. thick used for trussing, that is, bending the cask over a fire.

86 VICE (HEADING): see under Heading.

87 WET-STONE: large wheel-like stone turned by hand or treadle and running in a trough of water; used for sharpening tools.

Note: my friend Raphael A. Salaman's *Dictionary of Tools Used in the Woodworking and Allied Trades, c.* 1700-1970 (George Allen and Unwin Ltd., London, 1975) gives a very detailed and comprehensive catalogue of the coopers' tools.

Part Two
THE HISTORY
OF COOPERING

CHAPTER SIX

The Beginnings

In order to establish a clear and complete understanding of any subject it is advisable to go back to the beginning and study how and why it all started, but with coopering, as with many other ancient trades, we can go back so far that we inevitably find ourselves in the realms of conjecture. We must try to visualize those early men who, many thousands of years ago, roamed our green hills in search of the good life, and who in their searching discovered the rudiments of trades which were to form the basis of our economy until they eventually succumbed to the machine. We must try to fit together the meagre and scattered artifacts of flint, pottery clay, metal and wood which have come down to us, and reconstruct the primitive lives of our ancestors, assembling the pattern of discoveries and inventions which led to such revolutionary change, and ultimately to the blessing of posterity.

Ten thousand and more years ago prehistoric man, when his day's struggle for survival was over, might have found time to burn out the inside of an old tree trunk to use it as a vessel in which to store his victuals. He would probably finish off the inside shaping with his flint hand-axe or adze before making it smooth with a small, cleverly-made flint scraper. This vessel would have advantages over a baked clay pot in that it would be less easily broken, and a large storage vessel would be very necessary in a community dependent upon the occasional luck of the hunt.

One of the difficulties which prehistoric man would encounter with this vessel would be the shrinking and subsequent cracking of the sides when kept in a dry place, or left in the sun, and in order to rectify this he would need to cut thin pliable shoots of hazel and bind them round the trunk. At this stage we can see (fig. 48) the rudiments of a tub, bin or bucket.

From this crude beginning there might well have developed the germ of an idea, to be seized upon by the first shipwrights, who hollowed and shaped logs to make the first boats. A number of these have been

48. (*Left*) The rudiments of a tub.

49. (*Right*) Adzes taken from the Maikop barrow, Russia.

found, but little else in the way of wooden articles. However, with regard to the tools that were developed during this embryonic stage in the establishment of trades we have a much better record.

We have ample evidence of the skill of the knappers, who shaped the flint stones, and who insisted on using the best-quality flint, specially mined at places like Grimes Graves, in Norfolk. The flint was eventually superseded by copper and bronze, but tool designs continued, as is evident in fig. 50, where a typology of the axe shows how tradition caused the development of the common palstave axe. Excellent adzes, made in the conventional style with a hole for a shaft, and dating from the copper age, were found in the Maikop Barrow of South Russia, looking so much like present-day tools as to make one doubt their antiquity (fig. 49). A study of these two figures emphasizes, on the one hand, the power of traditional practice, and on the other hand, (and we might recognize this in retrospect in other facets of our story), how perhaps a spark of inventive genuis could put the clock forward a thousand years.

The adze was always a popular tool since a great degree of accuracy could be attained by a skilled man using it (*pl. 55*). It was the symbol used to designate the Ancient Egyptian Royal Architect, and a favourite tool of the Pyramid Age, 4000 BC.

It was with tools such as these that the early coopers toiled. Eventually they rectified the faults of the solid tub—weight and porosity—by making a taper on the trunk so that, by forcing hoops of hazel over the

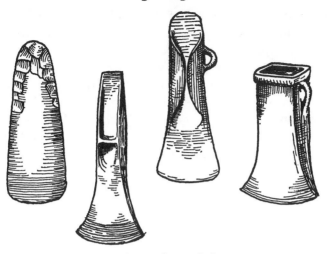

50. A typology of the axe.

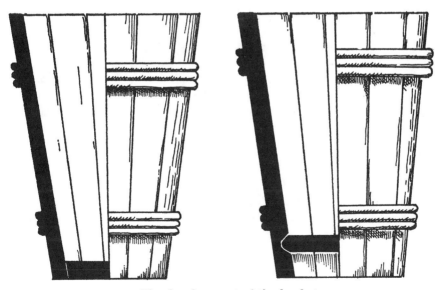

51. The development of the bucket.

smaller end, the cracked pieces of the trunk could be held tightly together, and a disc of wood could be fitted firmly in the bottom, in place of the porous end-grain of the trunk.

During the Bronze Age chisels were made which were capable of cutting grooves into the bottom of tubs. With these the coopers would be able to make a much more efficient article, but in order to get this disc, or head, into the tub the sides would have to be forced outward. It would soon occur to the cooper that individual staves could be cut in such a way as to be thin and still relatively impervious. And so

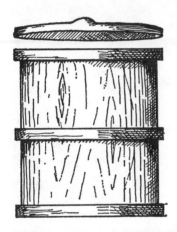

52. (*Left*) An early Egyptian wooden tub.

53. (*Below*) Ancient Egyptian wooden tubs.

we have the development of the bucket (fig. 51).

The photograph at (*pl. 51*) is of a bronze bucket found in a barrow grave at Vace Carniola, Yugoslavia, dating from the early Iron Age, and is undoubtedly based on the wooden bucket which must, by then, have been in common use.

Some of the earliest coopering of which we have evidence appears in rock carvings in the ancient tombs of Egypt. Egypt lacks a good workable timber, and clay vessels were used extensively in their small breweries, but a wall-painting in the tomb of Hesy-re, dating back to 2690 BC, showed a wooden tub and striker used for measuring corn; the staves are held together with wooden hoops (fig. 52). Fig. 53 is a drawing of a wall-painting taken from the tomb of Beni Hasan, 1900 BC, and shows raisins being stored in conventionally shaped tubs.

To make the first barrel the early coopers might have considered fitting a head into the top and bottom of a tub, but this would prove to be an awkward vessel, particularly when trying to move it about, and the idea presented, perhaps, by the appearance of two buckets, one upside down on top of the other, might well have been the inspiration needed to help them to visualize and create the barrel. They would need to shape and bend staves by fire, a technique already understood by the accidental bending and setting of boughs of trees across their fires. Now they could apply this hitherto perhaps useless or at most amusing knowledge to develop the ideal container.

It is from the Iron Age that we have the first evidence of barrels being used. Herodotus of Halicarnassus, that much-travelled Greek historian, wrote of palm tree wood casks being carried in curious circular ships down the river to Babylon around 800–900 BC. In the first book of Kings of the *Bible*, Chapter 18, Verse 33, it tells how, in the time of King Ahab of Israel, in the ninth century BC, the prophet Elijah defeated the priests of Baal. Three times he filled four barrels of water and poured them over a burnt offering. In the same book a widow had a 'handful of meal in a barrel'.

A tenable hypothesis, based on sound evidence, might be made out for the case that a sealed container, or barrel, was first constructed in districts where preservable drinks were brewed; they would be needed in the wine-growing areas where, at harvest times, considerable quantities of drink were fermented.

Edward Hyams put forward a reasoned argument that casks would not have been used extensively in Middle Eastern countries because of the difficulty of keeping them in sound condition in very hot, dry weather. Because of this the cheap palm-wood casks of Babylon were most probably broken up after one journey. In the Royal Navy some 2,000 years later it was a custom to fill wine and spirit casks with salt water as soon as they became empty, as a precaution against fire, but this would also keep the casks from drying out and falling apart.

There is no doubt that it was an understanding of how to smelt iron that made it possible to make vastly superior tools, capable of shaping the harder woods necessary for making liquid-carrying barrels. With these iron tools techniques were able to be perfected, and indeed these have continued, with slight modifications, right up to the present century. The iron tools at fig. 54, found at Thebes in Egypt, and said to originate in Assyria in the eighth century BC, illustrate the fact that designs have not altered tremendously except in respect of modern powered tools. It is interesting to note that among these early Assyrian tools there is a drilling bit intended for use in a wooden brace. The earlier way of making a hole was to use an old bow drill (*pl. 52*), and these were still used in Roman times, although by then the auger, a drill at the end of a tapered scoop, may well have been coming into use. Until breweries started to insert brass bushes in the bung and tap holes of casks early this century, these holes were always enlarged by burning them with a red-hot tapered iron rod. This was also said to prevent the wood from rotting. The idea most probably originated in the Iron Age, when it was the practice to shape wood roughly by burning.

Iron was a very expensive commodity during the Iron Age, and

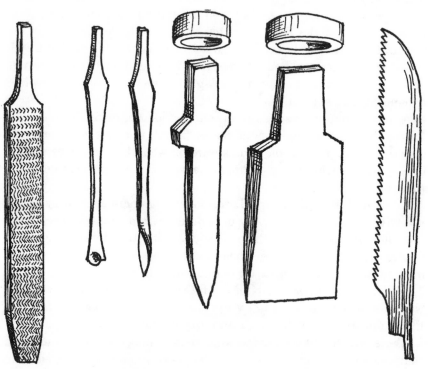

54. Eighth-century BC Assyrian iron tools.

indeed right up until the Industrial Revolution, and therefore it was customary to fit small cutting irons on to basically wooden tools. Specialist toolmakers were few, and local blacksmiths would be called upon to make the varied parts of tools based on ideas passed by word of mouth. Consequently we have numerous variations of tools bearing quaint names that differ all over the country, synonymous with old trades.

The processes and techniques which were developed at this time are basically those described in Part 1, Chapter 1. They became trade secrets, closely guarded and kept within families, small tribes and later guilds, passing down from father to son and from master to apprentice, right up to the present day.

Worn-out buckets and casks would be of little value, and would be left to fall apart and rot, but some of the earliest examples of coopering have come down to us preserved in the lake villages of Europe. The Friesch Museum at Leewarden in Holland possesses a number of large casks, six to seven feet long but only two to three feet in diameter, bound with wooden hoops, which were used in the artificial islands, or *terpen*, to protect the sides of wells, just as brickwork is today; two or three casks were sometimes used on top of one another. These date from about 200 B C.

The Lake (or lakeside) Village near Glastonbury, dating from the late Iron Age, just prior to the Roman occupation, gave up a number of wooden staves, plus one complete tub measuring 7 in. across and $6\frac{1}{4}$ in. high, with three staves at almost regular intervals left 2 in. proud at the bottom to form legs (fig. 55). The tub has twelve oak staves of about $\frac{1}{2}$ in. thickness. The most interesting thing about the tub is that the staves are dowelled together with wooden pegs, 1 in. long and a little more than $\frac{1}{8}$ in. thick (fig. 56). A tub made with its staves dowelled together would stay in position without hoops, even though in the making of it hoops would have been used to clamp it firmly into position. It would have made an admirable fruit bowl, or served a number of household needs, the standard of workmanship being very high. The stave in fig. 58 is $30\frac{1}{2}$ in. long, and was part of a vessel, possibly a churn, of $9\frac{1}{2}$ in. internal diameter, made out of solid oak, but involving coopering techniques.

The Marlborough Vat (*pl. 62*), is a nineteenth-century reconstruction which followed a drawing of the vat made before the original wood disintegrated after being lifted from the place where it had lain for over two thousand years. The ornamental bronze work which once covered

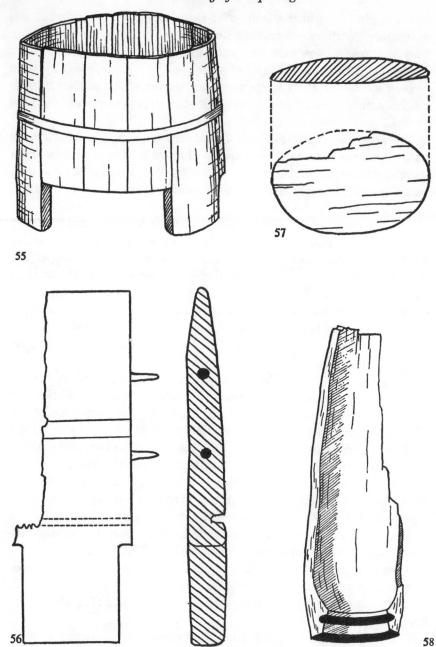

55. Wooden tub retrieved from Glastonbury lake village.
56. Dowelled stave excavated at Glastonbury lake village.
57. Piece of a cask head from Glastonbury lake village.
58. Part of a stave of a butter churn, Glastonbury lake village.

the outside of the vat has a Celtic-type embossing of circles and animals.

By the first century B C, barrels were being used for wines, beer, milk, butter and water, and buckets and tubs must have been commonplace.

A Belgic tribe, the Catuvellauni, which settled mainly in Hertford-shire and Essex, elevated the humble bucket to serve the purpose of a cremation urn. Excavated from one of their burials, the bucket (*pl. 52*) contained cremated bones and brooches. The Iron Age motifs embossed on the uppermost hoop are quite attractive, but although the wood has had to be reconstructed I am sure the cooper did justice to the honour paid to his trade.

It is not difficult to see the advantages which the coopered vessels had by comparison with the utensils which they were superseding. The clay jug was bulky, difficult to carry and easily broken, while animal skins often leaked and caused their contents to taste. The barrel in-volves the principle of the double arch, creating immense strength; it is in itself a wheel and a means of movement, and is not easily damaged. It was the container of the future.

CHAPTER SEVEN

The Roman Period

The cynic Diogenes, in order to abandon the vanities of desire for honour and comfort, to acquire wisdom and virtue, chose to live in a tub. Many interpretations featuring contemporary barrels (a medieval one is shown at *pl. 57*) have given Diogenes fame in excess of his life's work.

If confinement within a tub has the power of enlightenment it is more than the most boastful cooper would claim for his product. But in fact it was not a wooden cask which served Diogenes as a hermitage, but a clay *dolia*, made to hold over 120 gallons, and strengthened with wooden hoops; the wooden cask was not used by the early Greeks and Romans.

Gaius Plinius Secundus, the Roman historian, ignoring Herodotus, wrote that coopering had originated in the Alpine valleys and that the Gauls kept their beverages in wooden casks bound with hoops. Pliny wrote of the *Vietor Doliarius* (cooper), the *Vietor Vinarius* (wine cooper), the *Doliarius* (a cooper of great casks) and the *Vietor* (a basketmaker). A *Dolium* was a great vessel, and if it were *Doliaris* it was potbellied. A *Cupula* was a maker of *Cupa vel Cuppa* (butts, pipes or vats), and to hoop a cask was called *Vieo*. A *Testa* was a cask, a *Cadus Salsamentarius* a salting tub. *Cupae*, large empty vessels, were used, says Pliny the younger, in order to bear up the hulls of ships when they were careened in order that their hulls could be scraped or repaired, the dry dock of the Roman Era.

The security established by the Roman Legions and their wonderful roads enabled 'Human life to profit by the exchange of goods', according to Pliny the Elder. Later historians, notably A. H. M. Jones, referring to the absence of tariffs, have called it a vast common market. In these trading conditions the Romans soon found it expedient to make casks in Rome. This logical argument is reinforced by archaeological evidence which, because of the decomposing nature of wood, and therefore of any ancient coopering, is of a negative nature. The pottery

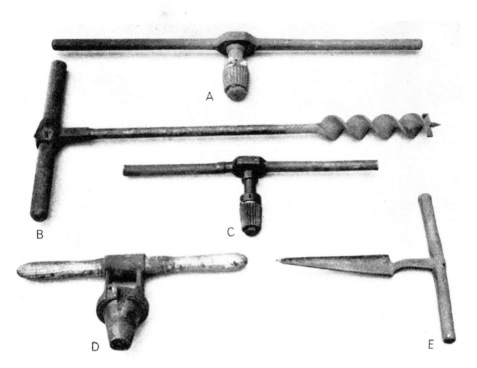

45. Bung-hole bushing tackle (A), large auger (B), keystone bushing tackle (C), flush borer (D), tapered auger (E)

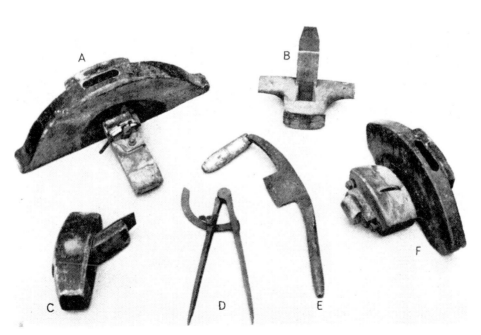

46. Croze (A), inside shave (B), stoup plane (C), compasses (D), jigger (E), chiv (F)

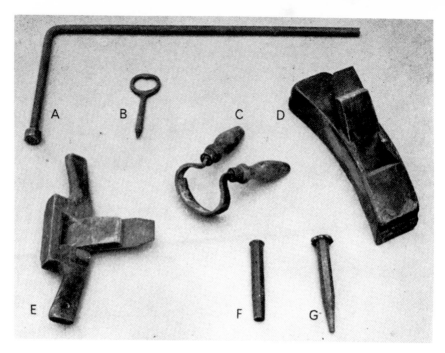

47. The knocker-up (A), heading vice (B), round shave (C),
topping plane (D), downright (E), rivet mould (F),
hoop punch (G)

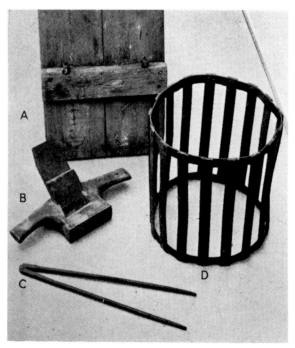

48. Heading board (A), swift (B), diagonals (C), cresset (D)

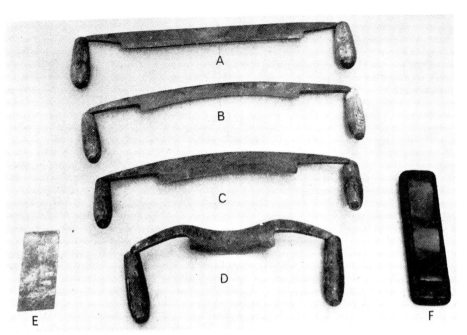

49. Backing knife (A), draw knife (B), heading knife (C),
hollow knife (D), scraper (E), oil stone (F)

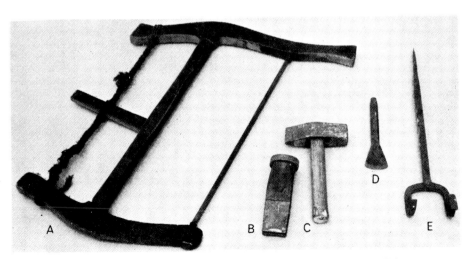

50. The bow saw (A), driver (B), hammer (C), chince (D),
flagging iron (E)

52. The Aylesford Bucket, Iron Age Britain

51. Bronze bucket, Early Iron Age

54. The Long Wittenham Stoup (approx. ⅔ actual size)

53. The Mountsorrel Bucket

55. Using an adze to convert a tree trunk

56. Using a bow-drill

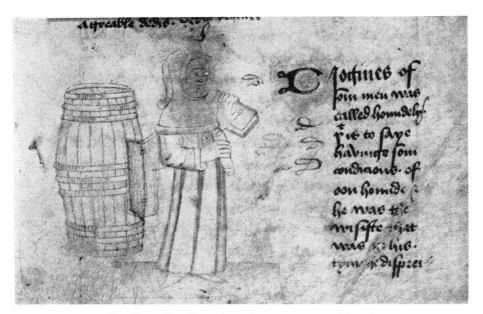

57. A medieval version of Diogenes and his tub

58. Roman casks from Silchester

59. The Trawsfynydd Tankard

60. The Trawsfynydd Tankard—a turned head in the bottom

vessels used for wine in southern vineyards, now dug up as broken 'potsherds', become scarce at intervals from AD 100 in Burgundy to AD 300 in more southerly latitudes, signifying, without doubt, the introduction of wooden casks into these areas.

Industry in the Roman towns and cities was carried on by small independent craftsmen, helped by their families and sometimes by apprentices and a few slaves or hired assistants. There were some slave establishments owned by well-to-do proprietors, but these were few. Trades tended to be hereditary, just as they have been to this day, and were organized in guilds called *Collegia Fabrorum*. These were corporate bodies recognized by Roman law. Each had a president and a treasurer, and could hold property. They had a common worship, in some cases a priest, and *Lares*, household gods, and *Genii*, protecting deities. These *Collegia* possessed certain insignia, held feasts and subscribed towards

59. Casks portrayed on Trajan's column, Rome.

the funeral and burial expenses of their members. Just as with the later guilds, they were used by local and Imperial authorities for such diverse purposes as the collection of *corvées*, money, and compulsory services such as the cleaning of drains, the re-erecting of columns and providing a fire brigade. The purpose of the Roman Guilds was not to press for more pay, better conditions or even higher status; their aims were strictly limited, and when some did engage in political activity, as in 64 BC, they were immediately banned; the Senate would brook no pressure group emanating from this source. The Roman authorities tended to control prices and regulate trade practices for the benefit of the customer, and the reason for this may be explained by Cicero when he states that trade was regarded as being below the dignity of the better-class Romans. It may be that this attitude jeopardized the development of Hero's steam engine, and the possibility of a Roman industrial Revolution, which would have cut short the life of our own and a vast number of other trades.

Fig. 59 shows a detail from Trajan's column in Rome, depicting casks being loaded on to a river boat, in A D 98. An Italian, Ciacono, writing in 1667, made the observation that these port-pipe-shaped casks were, 'just like those now in use everywhere'. The *Nicholson Encyclopaedia* of 1809 went further, saying that, 'The description given by writers on rural economy in Rome 2,000 years ago, as to the construction of casks, corresponds in good measure with that of our day.'

A bas relief on a Roman monument at Noviogamus near Trier, of the first century A D, depicts a Roman ship with a cargo of wine in casks on the Rhine (fig. 60). The Romans were great wine-drinkers, but they

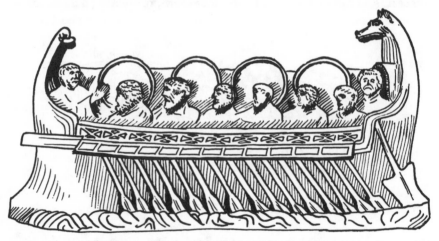

60. Wine casks on the Rhine, first century A D.

favoured the use of two-handled clay amphorae holding five gallons, and three-handled clay pitchers for their best wines. This might well have been because most of the casks which have come down to us from this period were made of silver fir, which would not have caused the maturing wine to improve in taste. Whether it was because of tradition, the softness of the wood, the inferior nature of the tools or the fact that other woods had not been experimented with, or were not so easily available where the casks were made, we do not know. Strabo, the Roman geographer of the first century A D, wrote of how wooden *pithoi* were lined with pitch. This was common practice with pottery vessels which were pitched to help preserve the wine. It would form a barrier stopping the taste of the wood from impairing the flavour of the wine, as well as preventing porousness. Eventually, when the maturing properties of oak were realized, this wood practically monopolized the wine industry and the 'barbarous' custom of pitching, stopping oxygenation of the wine through the pores of the wood, was not necessary. Until recently casks made of inferior, slight timber, and many dry-work casks, have been lined with pitch, paraffin wax, rubber and plastic solutions of a non-toxic nature.

The origin of the word cooper is said to stem from the wine-makers of Illyria and Cisalpine Gaul, where the wine was stored in wooden vessels called *cupals*, and the maker of these vessels was called a *cuparius*. The Middle Low German word *kufer*, or *kuper*, was derived from this, and similarly the English word 'cooper'.

Casks, which have been such a boon to man in his more mundane tasks, have also been utilized as a weapon of war and as a means of punishment. In 250 BC, Regulus, the commander of the Roman Army invading Carthage, after some initial successes was defeated and taken prisoner with 15,000 of his men. Carthage sent him to Rome to arrange terms, and put him on his honour to return. Back in Rome Regulus told his countrymen not to accept terms. He returned to Carthage where he is said to have been put to death by being confined in a barrel fitted inside with sharp iron spikes, and being rolled. This cruel method of execution was used on numerous occasions throughout history.

Julius Caesar, who described his military tactics to his own advantage, wrote of how he used tar barrels to start a conflagration in a town.

Maximin, the giant tyrant barbarian, who usurped the Roman throne, while besieging Aquileia in AD 238, brought large quantities of wine in wooden casks the size of hogsheads (54 gallons) for his army, and when they were empty he used them to make a pontoon bridge to enable his army to cross the flooded river and attack the city.

The oldest casks to have been unearthed in this country date from this period. In 1897, during excavations at Roman Silchester, casks were found which had served as linings for shallow wells, exactly as did the casks in the Dutch *terpen*. These were made of Pyrenean silver fir of one and a half inches thickness, with grooves where the heads of the casks had once been fitted when the casks had been used for wine at some time or other. One of the most revealing facts about these casks is that the Roman numerals had been scratched on the inside of each stave. With new casks it is not necessary to number staves as each stave is made to fit against any other, but after a cask is fired fibres squeeze and press into each other unevenly so that, if the cask needs to be taken apart and reassembled, it is necessary to keep the staves in the same order for the joints to match; hence the need to number them. The Romans were able to ship wine down the Rhine, across the Channel and into the port of Londinium, and would have been able to transport wine up the Thames to Silchester quite easily. Was it a bureaucratic slip that caused them to import these casks in shooks, with the staves in bundles to be reassembled, or were they 'knocked down' at some other time in their lives? *Pl. 58* shows three of the well casks excavated at Silchester.

The remains of two large Roman casks were discovered about 30 ft. below ground-level during excavations in London for the extension of the Bank of England in the early 1930s. These date from the second century A D at which time the River Walbrook ran under the site and barges carrying wine used the river. The larger cask was 78 in. long with an external head diameter of 28–30 in., and in the bulge 37–39 in. The width of the staves varied from 5 to $7\frac{1}{2}$ in. in the bulge and they were of 1 in. thickness. The cask would probably have contained between 230 and 240 gallons and been called a double *Culeus*, a *Culeus* being a 115-gallon cask, identical in size to the port pipe of today. The heads and the hoops had long since rotted away and the staves had fallen apart, but the position of the hoops could be made out quite clearly. They were made of pine wood, and while the external surfaces of the staves were somewhat decayed, the interior surfaces were in a much better state of preservation due to the impregnation of wine of considerable alcoholic strength. From the position and the number of tap and spile holes, one cask had been used upright and lying and been filled many times, and had probably made many journeys. The cooper had stamped his name clearly on the inside of one of the staves, *Cavisti*; the name *Pacati* and other names have been found on similar casks. The custom that coopers should mark their own work has continued up to the present day, and more will be said of this. The smaller cask had been cut down by 24 in. and its internal surface was considerably decayed, indicating that, like the Silchester casks, it had been used to line a well.

It is interesting to note that no locally made casks appear to have been used for wells. This strengthens the arguments regarding the origin of coopering, but since the British national drink was ale, the barley grain figured on their first coins, and since this could be brewed all the year round and did not need a long period of maturation, there was not the need for large casks in Britain.

The Mountsorrel bucket (*pl. 53*) was unearthed while excavating a Roman settlement around *Ratae*, Leicester, and dates from the fourth century A D. It was made with six oak staves, but was exceptional for the quality of its metalwork, suggesting an ornamental or religious purpose rather than a domestic one.

Pls. 59 and *60* show a tankard, cooper-made, and sheathed in bronze with a fine Celtic-style handle. It had ten staves and stood 5½ in. high with a capacity of 3 pints. The little head was turned on a lathe. It is from Merioneth, Wales, and dates from the first century A D, Iron Age B.

CHAPTER EIGHT

The Anglo-Saxon Period

The history books tell us how the legions left Britain to the tender mercies of numerous barbarian peoples, out of which, eventually, grew England. Trade was disrupted, and much of the economy reverted to a level of subsistence, but in the small towns and villages the old trades continued, their praises unsung.

The Anglo-Saxons drank considerable quantities of ale, and the Venerable Bede wrote that the Church often had cause to complain about the extent of drunkenness. The monks made no secret of the fact that they preferred wine, still being imported into this country from Germany in large relief-band amphorae, to the English wines introduced into this country by the Romans. Amphorae from Bordeaux were imported prior to A D 250, when they ceased abruptly, presumably superseded by wooden casks.

Ale had always been the staple drink of this country. Rents to the church were paid wholly or partly in kind, and in these ale figured prominently. Sesters of ale and Church Mittans of ale indicated a particular size of cask of which we know little; vats of honey are mentioned, and a cask container called an Amber, used for ale and butter.

A reminder of the drinking habits of these rough and hardy people can sometimes be found in their cemeteries in the form of very beautiful little drinking-vessels. One of these is the Long Wittenham Stoup (*pl. 54*), now in the British Museum. The four drinking-vessels (*pl. 61*) are lodged in the Ashmolean Museum in Oxford under the Latin name of *situlae*. The wooden staves of these have been partly or completely reconstructed in plaster, but even so they illustrate well the quality of craftsmanship of the Anglo-Saxon coopers. The vessel on the left stands 6 in. high and the others are correspondingly smaller. These stoups were made of individual staves of oak, yew or pine, and cut to between ¼ in. and ½ in. thickness. They must have been jointed with quite exceptional accuracy in order to hold liquid. A man's stoup was treated with considerable respect by the Anglo-Saxons. The Kings of

Kent issued a series of laws in the seventh century stipulating that, 'If where men are drinking, one man takes away the stoup of another, who had committed no offence, he shall pay, in accordance with established custom, a shilling to him who owns the house, six shillings to him whose stoup has been taken away, and twelve shillings to the King.' One must admire the sentiment displayed by these drunken pagan warriors in placing a dead man's stoup beside his body, and most probably filling it with a last drink of farewell. The dead could not be contemplated as being wholly spiritual, and, as well as libations, larger vessels, containing food for an after life, have also been exhumed from Anglo-Saxon graves.

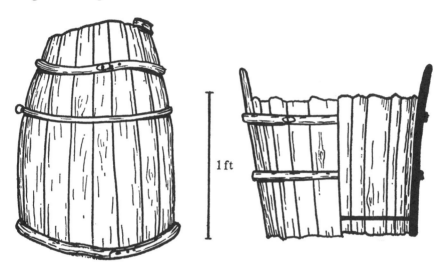

61. Irish churn and bucket, tenth century A D.

Churns and buckets dating from the tenth century have been excavated from the crannogs, the lake villages of Ireland and Scotland, and coopered vessels from this period are sometimes dug out of the peat bogs of Ireland (fig. 61).

The tools at (fig. 62) were found comparatively recently in a seventh-century Byzantine wreck on a dangerous reef at Yassi Island in the Eastern Mediterranean. The hammer, adze and chince, or caulking iron, could easily be mistaken for present-day cooper's tools, and are evidence of the high standard reached in the making of tools.

In 1939 at Sutton Hoo in Suffolk, among the richest treasure ever uncovered in the British Isles, that of the wealth and pride of an Anglo-Saxon King for whom an elaborate rowing-boat had been buried

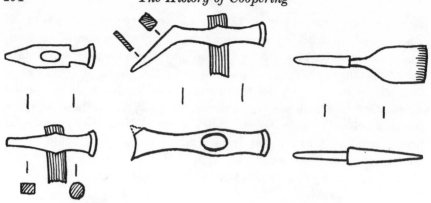

62. Hammer, adze and chince, seventh century A D.

as a cenotaph, were found a few very rusty iron hoops, handles and wrought-iron work. The butt (*pl. 63*) together with a smaller one, was reconstructed in plaster, and is presumed to have held food for the dead king. It stands almost 2 ft. high, strong and purposefully built rather than ornamental.

The Vikings possessed fine coopers. A large keg for holding the water supply and a wooden bucket were found in the Gokstad ship, excavated at Sandar near Oslo Fiord in 1880, and three finely made butts, one having held wild apples, and two wooden pails, were unearthed in the Oseberg ship dating from the ninth century. It is interesting to note that ceramics, which had been skilfully practised in Norway up to the age of the Vikings almost disappeared during the Viking Age. Pottery was mostly replaced by wooden vessels, soap-stone pots and iron cauldrons. The development of coopering would seem inevitable among a people living in a country having a plentiful supply of timber and needing large, strong containers for their provisions at sea. This is another instance where shipbuilding and coopering developed side by side.

Wooden braces, similar to the coopers' braces, into which scoop-bits were fitted for boring holes, have come down to us from the Viking Age, and, no doubt, these clever woodworkers must have stimulated activity in coopering in this country. Statutes of Anglo-Saxon Guilds have come down to us from the tenth century, but these were Thames' Guilds, an insurance against being killed by ensuring a vendetta against the murder; a Knights' Guild (they 'drank their gild and held it freely,' in Winchester) and a Peace Guild under the presidency of a bishop, established in order to help suppress theft. But in the growing towns tradesmen were able to congregate and specialize, and it was natural that they too should soon start to form their own guilds.

The Early Medieval Period

Norman influence, following the conquest, resulted in an increasing amount of wine being shipped into the country in tuns, large casks holding over two hundred gallons. One such tun was portrayed on the famous Bayeux Tapestry (fig. 63). The trade naturally flourished after the marriage of Henry II to Eleanor of Aquitaine, which brought Gascony under English rule. By the fourteenth century and prior to 1337 it was not unusual for as much as 20,000 tuns of wine per year to be imported into Bristol alone from Bordeaux and Bayonne.

All manner of tubs and casks were used in wine-making (*pl. 64*) for although the wine press had been invented and worked by levers in the days of the ancient Greeks, and by a screw thread in the time of the Romans, grapes were still trodden in open vats to extract the must. One is reminded of the words of Mendelssohn's Vintage Song,

> *On stave and hoop the long year through*
> *We worked with will and pleasure,*
> *And when the cask was firm and true,*
> *We pressed the vineyard's treasure.*

Many of the names of specialist tools used in coopering came into common use following the Norman conquest. The croze, used for cutting a groove, came from the old French word meaning hollow or groove; the brace is of Middle English origin, AD 1200–1500, coming from the Old French meaning two arms. The word bevel comes from the Old French; 'cresset' is of Middle English usage, originating from the Old French. The word 'barrel' came into use during this period and comes from the Old French word *baril*; 'butt' originates from the Old French *bot*. The origin of the word 'hogshead' is somewhat obscure, but the words 'kilderkin', 'firkin' and 'pin', all different sizes of casks, came into use during this period, and were from the Middle Dutch, thus indicating the extent to which the influence of the Dutch craftsmen and traders affected coopering in England. The names of many tools go back much further in history. The auger comes from the Old English word *nafu-gar*, the nave of a wheel and a piercer; the words 'axe' and 'adze' are old English of unknown origin. 'Dowel' is derived from the Middle Low German word *dovel* and came into general usage in this country during this period.

In almost all but the very smallest of towns merchants were organizing themselves into guilds. This was a natural development as a way of protecting themselves from outside competition by ensuring monopoly trading within their towns, and as an insurance for widows and orphans. In the ethics of medieval life scarcity and glut did not enter into the establishing of a just price, which was arrived at by custom,

TRAhVNT : CARRVM
CVMVINO : ETARM IS:

63. A wine tun from the Bayeux Tapestry.

and practices which were inconsistent with these ideals were discouraged or positively forbidden.

In its early days the merchant guild appeared to have had a wide membership so that the guild rolls of Leicester in 1196 include a variety of trades and professions including weavers, dyers, wool-combers, shearmen, tailors, hosiers, tanners, leather-workers, shoe-makers, saddlers, parchment-makers, soap-makers, leeches, preachers, mercers, goldsmiths, farriers, turners, coopers, potters, millers, bakers, cooks, butchers, watermen, masons, carpenters, plumbers, porters and ostlers.

Most trades were organized on a very small scale with a master man employing an occasional apprentice and at most one or two journeymen; only in the growing woollen trade were capitalist employers prevalent. The early Tax Rolls of 1292–1332 show that the bulk of apprentices in the city were country born and mostly from the home counties. The guilds fought successfully to ensure that upon having served a registered apprenticeship a man qualified for the freedom of the city, so that he belonged to the so-called enfranchized aristocracy. Aliens were able to buy membership of a company and so become citizens in this way, though there was much contention among gildsmen about this.

Tradesmen exhibited great pride in their work and were known by the name of the trade which they practized, as a prefix to their name, and as a mark of respect and courtesy. Upon getting married, and in order to get together the necessary utensils needed in the home, a young couple would pay a visit to Cooper So-and-So. According to Alexander Neckham, Abbot of Cirencester, who lived at the end of the twelfth century, numerous coopered vessels were used in the home. Many casks became valued possessions, and men would boast of casks which had been in the family for many years, and how a particularly noted and skilful cooper, perhaps long since dead, had made a certain cask. People would therefore choose their cooper and their casks very carefully.

For the kitchen pickling vats would be needed in a wide variety of sizes for all manner of foods to be preserved during the winter, as will as small flour barrels, similar to those illustrated at *pl. 65* and jugs somewhat larger than the ornamental one in the picture. Wooden bowls and buckets would be essential (*pls. 67, 68*), although the hoops would have been wooden; metal hoops were extremely expensive, and they would have been heavy and clumsy. When the new Guildhall opened in Reading in 1120 the speakers had difficulty in being heard over the noise being made by the washerwomen with their 'tubs and chatter', who were subsequently barred from rinsing clothes in the common stream. Such washing is well illustrated at *pl. 71*, taken from a sixteenth-century German calendar. The household book of Dame Alice de Bryere, 1412–13, contained a reference to an old pipe being cut in half as a tub for the laundress. Right up until the Second World War some women still used a worn-out beer cask holding about 18 gallons in which to wash clothes. This was called a dolly tub, and presumably the word derives from the Latin *doliaris*, meaning tubby, or *doliolum*, a small cask.

The poor medieval wife might also have been expected to tend the cows, the milking being done using a wooden bucket having one stave proud and used as a handle so that the other hand could be free to milk (fig. 64), and sitting on a three-legged stool; the Scots would say she had a creepie and leglin. She would also be expected to make butter and cheese in coopered tubs and churns. The dutiful wife would also brew ale for the whole family, as this was the staple drink, and for this she would need vats, casks and tubs. Perhaps because this came to be regarded as women's work it was natural for the alewife to run the ale-house.

64. The medieval milkmaid.

The Cowper or Cooper Street of many of our towns originated from these times. They were narrow and cobbled with a gutter running down the centre of the road. Craftsmen conducted their business from their dwelling-houses. These generally had a narrow frontage, and the room facing the street would be the workshop as well as the sales-shop. The cellar and sheds adjoining the house would also be workshops. Above the shop would be the solar, or family room, and behind the shop, the hall or living-room. The shop itself would be very small, perhaps only 6 × 15 ft., and sometimes part of that might be sub-let. Apprentices were bound to live with their masters, eating at their master's table, and more than likely sleeping in the workshop itself, for a period of seven years, beginning and ending on a certain saint's day. Things were made to order, but casual selling would be carried out from a booth in the market square on market day, which was often a Sunday, despite remonstrations from the church. The coopers of Coventry, together with the Turners, always held a market on Good Fridays, and their rights were upheld against the church's protests.

The monopoly privileges of the guilds, and the tolls imposed upon outsiders, enabled the guild merchants to become quite prosperous. They were now primarily merchants, and in order to maintain and strengthen their monopoly they sought to make it increasingly difficult for anyone to become a member of the guild, and financially crippling to join the livery. Discontent among the growing number of unfranchised craftsmen manifested itself in other forms of associations, namely the Craft Guilds.

England did not suffer the civil strife between the crafts and the older mercantile patriciate, as did the Continent. The mercantile misteries in London maintained control through the Aldermanic Court until 1327 when the new craft guilds started to buy charters from the king. But before the end of the thirteenth century crafts were being granted ordinances or condoned by the older guilds if they were regarded as inoffensive, or too poor to be troublesome. Those trades with a competitive mercantile element met with a hostile response. In 1298 the council, half of them representatives of newly emancipated industrial and victualling misteries, did not hesitate to break an attempt by the coopers to organize themselves. A reference in the *London Letter Book B* runs, '. . . came the coopers of the City . . . and made fine, each according to his ability, to the amount of thirty-one shillings. . . .' This was quite a considerable sum in those days, for when in 1310 the widow of Walter le Cuver, the surname having the practical significance of medieval custom, had her stock of casks seized because of bankruptcy, a barrel sold for 8d., a bucket for 3d., and four tubs for 5d. The coopers were soon to be centred on the Church of St Michael, Bassishaw, now no more, though the site is still called Coopers Corner, next to the Old Guildhall. We do not know exactly why the council took this attitude towards the coopers, although we do know that they had imposed oaths and applied ecclesiastical sanctions, including excommunication, on recalcitrants, as was then common practice, but it also happened to be one of the reasons for the council's longstanding hostility towards the Ecclesiatical Courts; it was thought that the church tended to transform the passive craft guild into the aggressive mistery. The Mayor of London's Court Rolls record a number of craft formations at the turn of the century. As well as coopers there were smiths, chandlers, barbers, brewers, spurriers and fruiterers exhibiting a spirit of solidarity, and applying for recognition. This is regarded by some historians as a product of the petty-bourgeois medieval system with its mathematical distribution of power; but with people to whom serfdom outside the towns was a reality there would have been a need for this kind of emotional and social security. The guilds provided an insurance against ill-health and unemployment, and security for widows, ensured a fair price for a job which met the guild standard, limited the number of apprentices so as not to overstaff the trade, and, made sure that they were sufficiently well trained by insisting on the production of a masterpiece. There was, of course, the very strong religious foundation. Above all the guildsmen were assured of a monopoly of trade within their town, as all outsiders were barred. As late as Tudor times, in 1529, we can find an entry in the Coventry Leet Book of a sitting under the judgement of the Mayor, Thomas Astelene, which reads,

Whereas one Thomas Reives of Berkeswell wekelie selleth Cowpers wares within this Citie beyng unlawfull stuff and disceavablie maid havyng a shope at the Spicers Stoke (South of Butchers Row) wherein all his wares do lie; which Thomas beireth no manner of Charges with the Craft of Cowpers of this Citie; wherfor it is enacted that the seid Reives shall not occupie eny shop within this Citie oneles he agre with the Cowpers of this Citie; and it is further provided that the seid Cowpers shall not take for eny agrement or fyne of the seid Reives above ij s. a yeire. . . .

The Coopers of Leith in Scotland received an 'Act of the Council of Edinburgh . . . that no outland cooper or stranger should be suffered to work either in house, close or booth in Leith except such as are lawfully admitted'. The Glasgow coopers ensured that '. . . nane of the said craftismen in ony tyme cumming sett up buiths nor pretend to work at his one hand bot he be maid first burgess and freman of the said burgh and be examinal be foure or sex of the perfytest men of the said Craft being Maisteris gif he be qualifeit and hable . . .' And similar laws were passed by the guilds in all large towns and cities.

Extracts from ancient writings give evidence of the use of barrels for transporting goods. In 1158, Chancellor Becket went to France to demand a princess in marriage for Prince Henry. 'He prepared lavishly to display the wealth of English luxury', wrote his chaplain, William Fitzstephen, '. . . two chariots were laden solely with iron-bound barrels of ale.' The fact that the barrels were specifically described as iron-bound, in contrast to the more common wooden-bound barrels, is a clear indication of the value attached to iron.

Coins were shipped in barrels, and the origin of the phrase, 'Scraping the bottom of the barrel', although somewhat obscure, might well have first been used at this time.

By the time of the Crusades wooden casks were the standard means of transporting all manner of liquids and provisions, and the cooper was coming into his own as one of the foremost tradesmen, particularly in coastal and riverside towns. This was so on the Continent, and a census of the master men of the guilds of Nuremberg, Germany, taken in the year 1363, shows by comparison the relative numerical importance of certain trades in an important and busy riverside trading town. It gives, Shoemakers 81, Tailors 76, Bakers 75, Cutlers 73, Butchers 71, Leatherworkers 60, Furriers 57, Tanners 35, Coopers 34, Dyers 34, Tinkers 33, Clothiers 28, Locksmiths 24, Farriers 22, Coachbuilders 20, Hatters 20, Toolmakers 17, Saddlers 16, Carpenters 16, Plasterers 14, Glaziers 11, Potters 11, Painters 6.

Plate 70 shows the Old Guildhall at Leicester, typical of the gathering-places of the guildsmen, and where local government had its roots, and the mayor gave his judgement upon the conduct of local affairs.

All our English liberties, or what is left of them, have been won by the town tradesmen. Thomas Burke quotes Green in saying,

In the silent growth and elevation of the English people the boroughs led the way. . . . The rights of self-government, of free speech in free meetings, of equal justice by one's equals, were brought safely across the ages of tyranny by the burghers and shop-keepers of the towns. In the quiet, quaintly-named streets, in town-mead and market place, in the bell that swung out its summons to the crowded borough-mote, in merchant-gild and church-gild and craft-gild, lay the life of Englishmen who were doing more than knight or baron to make England what she is. . . . Charter after charter during Henry's reign raised the townsmen of boroughs from mere traders, wholly at the mercy of their lord, into customary tenants, who had purchased their freedom by a fixed rent, regulated their own trade, and enjoyed exemption from all but their own justice.

CHAPTER TEN

The Late Medieval Period

Until the Tudors brought strong centralized government to England, units of weight, measurement and capacity varied from town to town, just as today they vary from country to country, and since the cask was used for all manner of goods it was inevitable that its capacity would be the subject of legislation. Guilds were aware that status could only improve with standards, and were pleased to comply with detailed regulations and become the instruments of city government to that end. A proclamation of 1382 stated that coopers were '. . . to make and buy gallons, potels, quarts and gills of good and lawful size'. With these pewter and wooden measures larger casks could be gauged, and sizes standardized.

It was to their mutual advantage that the coopers and the Billingsgate fishmongers co-operated effectively at this time. In 1413 a certain Richard Bartlott, a fishmonger, clandestinely made 260 fish casks in the cellar of his dwelling-house. Richard's enterprise was soon discovered, and the coopers were outraged at this infringement of their monopoly. Upon demand they were granted the right of search, and found that the casks were '. . . . made of impure woods, sawn from the middle', probably of unseasoned wood incorrectly cut, so that it would shrink and warp. The barrels were found to hold only 28 gallons instead of 30, and the firkins held only $6\frac{1}{2}$ gallons instead of $7\frac{1}{2}$. Richard's casks were seized, taken to the Guildhall, viewed, certified false and publicly burned.

In 1396, in order to improve the standards within the mistery, and thereby to eliminate unfair competition, an application was made by '. . . the good men of the mistery of coopers', to the Mayor and Aldermen of the City of London for an ordinance to restrain those of the mistery from making vessels for beer or other liquors out of oil or soap tuns, 'for the avoidance of such deceipts, for the love of God, and as a work of charity.' It is common practice for coopers to make small casks out of larger ones, and such casks are called 're-makers'; however it would be impossible to remove the smell of oil or soap because their fumes would penetrate deeply into the wood and so taint any liquor that it subsequently contained. Disreputable coopers must have persisted in defrauding their customers, for the coopers, jealous of their reputation, again petitioned the mayor for ordinances to put an end to these practices. It was consequently ordained in 1409 that no one of the mistery, living within the liberty of the City, should make any wooden vessels in which liquor ought to be put, unless of '. . . . pure and entire woods'. Re-making from wine casks would be quite an acceptable and profitable business, and with the wine trade flourishing empty wine casks would be cheap and plentiful.

Complaints about the capacity of casks have always been numerous and persistent since they have the most detestable habit of emptying rather too quickly. Because of the fact that they shrink in the course of wear they are always made oversize, but the brewer wisely sells a cask of beer, not a specified number of gallons. In 1420 an ordinance was passed stipulating that ale casks were to hold 30 gallons to the barrel, and 15 to the kilderkin, and beer casks 36 gallons to the barrel and 18 to the kilderkin, and these latter capacities appertain today. To ensure compliance with this ordinance every cooper was to have his own sign in iron and to brand every cask he made, and a record of his mark was to be kept at the Guildhall. Within fourteen days forty-six coopers within the franchise of the City brought their marks or brands of iron to the Guildhall, and they were duly placed on the records, which can be seen today (*pl. 72*). There was an earlier reference to coopers' marks being recorded at the Guildhall in 1407, but of this we know little regarding the outcome. However, most coopers of repute would be only too pleased to do this as an advertisement, and up to this century independent cooperages have branded their house-marks on their casks, and coopers have had their individual block mark stamped in the chime. In 1422 the coopers appointed wardens to supervise these rulings. Realizing that the shrinking of green timber was the main reason for short-measure casks, these wardens, supported by their members, petitioned for a further ordinance in 1428, regulating the trade by prohibiting the use of unseasoned timber.

In order to extend and consolidate its power the coopers' guild applied to the mayor in Common Council in 1440 to establish six points;

1. That no brewer or huckster should sell ale by barrel or kilderkin

unless bearing a proper cooper's mark, proving that barrels contained 30 gallons and kilderkins 15 gallons.

2. No cooper to make casks in the City of London unless he has been given a proper mark forged in iron.

3. When a cooper dies his iron to be taken to the Chamberlain of the City for the time being, to keep it out of the hands of evildoers.

4. That no man falsely counterfeit the marks of coopers.

5. That no cooper employ a foreigner or stranger until he has been brought by the wardens in front of the Mayor and Aldermen to prove he is an able workman. ('Foreigners' was the name given to people, or casks, originating from outside of the City but within this country, while the word 'strangers' was given to aliens or casks coming from abroad.)

6. That no cooper make a barrel for sweet wine unless it be 18½ gallon.

The wording of an ordinance, 36 Henry VI, of 1457, is worth repeating;

. . . for eschewing and voiding the grevous harme and grete deceit that nowe of late daies hath growen unto the commons of this Citee by diverse persons havyng no consideracon unto the saide orenaunce . . . to make untrue barrels . . . of sappie and unclene tymbre and of less mesures . . . Therefore the Mair and the aldermen . . . havying more special zele and tendre affeccion, as them oweth, unto the goode conservacon and avauncement of the comon wele and profit of the people than to any singuler avauntaige . . . that all suche vessels . . . here at this place shall be dampned and brent . . . so that all other may take a warnesse of making of any suche untrew and unclean vessels herafter.

A paragraph in an ordinance of 1488 concerning cask sizes and marks gives a clue to the readiness of the Mayor and aldermen to accede to the requests of the guilds. It reads, 'That oon half of all the saide fynes, forfeitures and penalties as of the auntages of markyns . . . to be applied to the use of the chambre of this Citee, and that the other half to the use of the saide crafte of Cowpers'. The 'special zele and tendre affeccion' was therefore well bolstered by financial self-interest.

As evidence of the continuing co-operation between the Coopers and Fishmongers of Billingsgate, and the seriousness with which they viewed practices detrimental to their trades, sixty casks for herrings were burnt in the presence of the Mayor at the Standard in Cheap in 1464, after a scrutiny by the wardens of both companies.

The Coopers fined members sums ranging from 8d. to 10s. in 1443 for selling defective casks, and again several coopers were amerced in 1444. Cooper Thomas Plaistowe marked nine foreign kilderkins with his iron mark and paid the chamberlain 6s. 8d. for his indiscretion. For having unmarked casks in their possession coopers could be fined quite heavily, and in 1490 the Mayor was petitioned to reduce the fine from a permissible 40s. to a more realistic 20d., which was granted.

The branding of casks with the cooper's mark was made compulsory by the guilds of most cities. Glasgow passed an ordinance in 1540, and in the time of James V a law was passed, '. . . that the Cowper and Town have Branding Irons for marking said barrells and what is not so marked to be escheat, half to the King, half to the Town'. The Coopers of Perth were made to '. . . burn on the tapen staff with particular merchant's marks'.

To a guild desirous of acquiring status within the small community the social aspects of guild life were important, and members were required to conform to a code of conduct. One can understand the feelings aroused when in 1443 five London coopers were taken before the Mayor for 'fighting violently in the presence of their wardens; they were adjudged to prison unless they paid their fines, . . . and so they paid them'. Cooper Richard Wrenne, for certain defaults, and particularly for abusing his wardens and calling them extortioners, was fined 6s. 8d. and ordered to go on his knees upon the ground and humbly beg remission of his wardens and all his brethren.

Many guild chantries were established with endowments so that priests could yearly upon the vigil make prayers for the dead; these were stopped and the moneys confiscated after the Reformation. The religious aspect of guild life was such that one cooper was fined 3 lb. of wax, worth, we are told, 12d., for not going to St Paul's Church 'at the instance and command of his masters'. The Coopers Company had its own altar in the old St Paul's Cathedral, with its own Chantry Priest to say requiems for departed members as well as celebrate their post orbits. The Coopers' Pall must have been a most elaborate and resplendent cloth, for it was made with 6½ lb. of gold and silver with all manner of silks at a cost of £56 9s. 1d. This, unused when the practice of corporate funerals ceased, was sold in 1678 to help towards the cost of a new hall.

The Coopers Company of Newcastle, in an ordinary dated 20

January 1426, stated that coopers were to go together yearly at the feast of Corpus Christi in procession with other craftsmen, and play their play at their own charge; each brother to attend at the hour assigned him on pain of forfeiting a pound of wax.

Saints' Days Pageants and religious festivals were expensive items, particularly to the Craft Guilds of Coventry. In the Leet of William Kemp, Mayor in 1459, the Coopers were 'joyned and associat unto ye Craftes of Carpenters and Pynners to be contributory frohensforth with theym in such charges as they yerely ber for the worship of yis Citie'. In 1542 the Coventry Tilers joined the Coopers, Pynners and Carpenters, a special reference being made to the fact that the Carpenters were to contribute their portion as accustomed in the past. The Carpenters were not included in a reference made in 1547 where it was enacted that the three trades, Tilers, Pynners and Coopers, should associate as in the past and that the 'Cowpers shal-be the hedd and cheffest of theym and stand charged with the pagyaunt'—a doubtful privilege. It was also decreed that no one could play in any craft pageant other than his own, so that every one could have the chance to participate. Mention is made of a sextary, a 14-gallon cask that was used in Coventry at this time.

The Coopers of York performed the same play at every pageant, 'Man's disobedience and fall from Eden'. There may have been some good reason for them to perform this particular play, for it was a cooper who, in 1483, stood up before the Lord of Gloucester's nominee for mayor of York and shouted, 'The commons will not have him as mayor', and talked himself out of it with the astuteness of a modern politician. The coopers were strongest in York around 1400 when it was still a thriving port. Between 1272 and 1306, two coopers were admitted to the Freedom, between 1307 and 1349 there were fourteen. The number doubled to twenty-eight between 1350 and 1399 and dropped to twenty-seven between 1400 and 1449, continuing to fall to nineteen between 1450 and 1509.

The Coopers of Shrewsbury who, together with the Fletchers and Bowyers, received their Charter by 27 Henry VI, 1449, would yearly go in procession to the Weeping Cross, two miles out of the town, where, 'all joined in bewailing their sins and in chanting forth petition for a plentiful harvest'. There followed a service in St Chad's Church and then three days of recreation.

In 1456 Cooper Swift of London procured casks from another member of the guild in order to resell them. He did not pay for these casks as agreed, but when pressed tried to pay in kind, 'for to take hit owte in ale, of lesse that he know verely that the man thet hath servyd hym before be full contendid and agreid. . . .' The case was taken to arbitration, and I quote the original wording . . .

This ys the award made by John Broune, Thomas Pope and Robert Ferryn, arbitratorz indifferently chosen, be twene John Noreys and Richard Hardgode, wardeyns of the crafte of Cowpers of London and William Swyft, Cowper, in the fest of Seynt the Martier, in the 35th. yere of Kyng Henry the VI. Fyrst we awarde that for the grete obstynacye and dyshobedyence of the seyde William agyns his seid wardeynes of all suche forfetez as he hath done theym; and beseche theym of theyre gode maystyrshippez; and also aske forgevenes of all the brethryn of the seyd crafte that he hath offended unto. And that he shall on his knee, but yif the wardens wyll yeve hym grace.

There was a steady growth in the membership of the London coopers' guild with a temporary setback around the middle of the century. In 1439 forty coopers were paying their dues, called quarterage, as it was paid quarterly; in 1443 fifty-one paid quarterage; in 1454 it had dropped by two to forty-nine, but by 1457 it had risen again to fifty-one, and in 1460 fifty-five were paying quarterage. Reference to the stagnation in trade during the late forties and fifties is contained in an ordinance of 1488 which states that foreigners and strangers were being employed, 'in no wyse therein expert ne connyng', so that coopers who had undertaken good apprenticeships now 'for lacke of accupacion become idoll and goo aboute wandryng this Citee, werkless as vagabunds', and others taught lads over whom they had no bond, 'certain feets and poynts' so that 'with that little connyng that they have taken, go into the cuntreie and there worke as well works unlawfull as of unseasonable tymbre, to the great deceipt of the king's liege people'.

In 1444 a cooper was fined for 'fraudulently' receiving an apprentice, and in the following year two members who employed a foreigner 'against the form of the art' were fined 6s. 8d. The Craft Wardens put into force strict rules as regards apprentices. They were to be presented to the wardens to ensure that they were 'free born of true kynrede, and reght and clene of lymmes, uppon payne of twenty shillings, and every apprentice twenty pence'. In 1491 there were twelve apprentices paying quarterage of 1s. 8d.

In 1488 the Coopers applied for an ordinance to more or less codify existing rulings. It read.

. . . That where grete deceit and untrowthe dayly been used within this Citee, by the means of makyng of barells, kilderkyns, firkyns and other vessells wheren licor shalbe put, of sappy and grene tymber, for lacke of serche and correccion theuppon to be hadde and done, the which vessells so made, after they have been any while occupied, of necessite must shrynke, wherethrugh the same vessells at the laste weryng of theym, lacke of their true and juste measure that they ought to conteyne, that is to say, somme of them iiij galons, somme iij galons, somme ij galons, somme more, somme less . . . . Also that no persone of the said crafte of Cowpers nor any other persones occupying the same craft within the said Citee of liberties thereof, hereafter make or do to be made any vessell for sope, but if the barell conteign and hold xxx galons, the half barell and firkyn after the saim rate; nor any vessel for bere, but if it keepe holde and conteyn the true and full measure of olde tyme accustomed that is to say, the barell xxxvi galons, the kilderkyn xviij galons and the firkyn ix galons at the leste; and that every such vessell be marked with a Cowper's marke entered in the chamber of theldhall of this Citee of record . . . .

By insisting upon high standards in their fight against outside competition the London coopers established a reputation for good quality work which they maintained through the centuries and for which they were renowned until their redundancy. With the cost of transporting goods being extremely high, prices could vary in different parts of the country, and London prices were always higher than most other prices. Therefore if a cooper were to leave the guild for some reason or other, he would find that by moving into the country to escape the guild's jurisdiction he would find himself the poorer financially.

Many coopers found employment with the Army Commissariat in times of war, as most supplies were contained in casks. English soldiers escorting a supply of food for the army beseiging Orléans would vouch for the strength and usefulness of barrels, for when they were intercepted by the French, their herring barrels proved such an effective palisade that they were able to repulse the attack and join the main army.

The punishment of rolling a culprit or victim in a cask through which long nails had been driven to leave the points protruding inside was not uncommon in medieval times. A famous sufferer was Gerhard van Velren who, according to the Dutch Chronicle, was punished for the murder of Count Florens V in 1296. In a song written in memory of the drama the words run, 'they rolled him there for three days long, three days before noontide', but when asked how he felt Gerhard was unrepentant. 'I am still the self-same man who took the life of the Count,' he replied.

Fig. 65 is a drawing from an old manuscript of 1355 showing how casks were used as buoyancy tanks by an ingenious inventor.

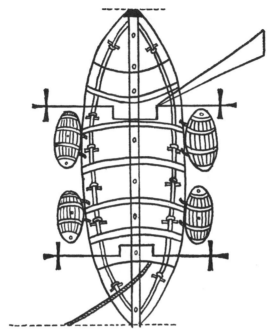

65. Casks used as buoyancy tanks, fourteenth century.

During the thirteenth century princes along the Rhine vied with each other to possess the largest wine cask. One might think this to be a very friendly and civilized way of establishing national prestige. The German coopers raised some wonderfully large and elaborately carved vessels, and people came from all over Europe to see them. In 1552 one of the princes was boasting that he possessed a cask capable of holding 100 fuders, or 22,000 gallons. The most famous of these vessels is the Heidelberg Tun. Raised in 1754, it holds some 49,888 gallons, and is the successor of two previous tuns, the first being built in 1591. It was made by Master-cooper Englert, who provided it with a gallery and a dancing floor, as can be seen in Plate 81. It is still on show in Heidelberg Castle. The German princes appointed Court Coopers, and within their palace building complex there was a Band House, or as we would say, a Coopers' Shop.

CHAPTER ELEVEN

The Tudor Period

'To all present . . . Equytie woll and reason ordeyneth that vertuouse men and of honest occupation bee by their merits remunered and rewarded in this worlde, and to be perpetuall memory for their good and vertuouse name and fame, and their successours aftir theym for evermore. . . .'

So runs the wording of the charter granting arms to the Coopers Company, 27 September 1509. The Charter itself was granted in 1501, when they were classed as a 'perpetual guild' with one master and two wardens or keepers of the Commonalty of Freedom of the Mistery of Cowpers, to

make lawful and honest meetings and make reasonable laws, statutes and ordinances, for the wholesome rule and government of the said mistery to the exingency of necessity as often as and when needed . . . so long as they be not against the laws and custom of the Kingdom of England and the Citee.

The arms are at *pl. 73*. The coopers' motto at that time was, 'Gaude Maria Virgo', but, like the Vicar of Bray, discretion took precedence over principle, and the motto was changed at the time of the Reformation to, 'Love as Brethren'. The camels, as in the Grocers' Arms, signified trade, and the rings unity. It is possible that the tools portrayed were drawn in error, as they appear to be a mallet and two woodchoppers' axes. In later printed papers and on the heading of an account of 1575 the mallet is clearly a croze, and the two axes are coopers' axes, and later representations show these tools quite distinctly. The large rings on the shield, annulets, represent hoops.

In the same year as they were granted arms the coopers attended as one of the livery companies in the procession for the funeral of Henry VII from Richmond, through the City to Westminster Abbey. They supplied their proportion of torches and of poor men dressed in white gowns and hoods. Ten of the principal City Companies were also required to prepare from one to twelve of their members to attend on horseback clothed in black gowns and tippets. The coopers were required to send two. A space of 6 yards in Cheapside was allocated to the coopers at the coronation of Henry VIII.

It has not been ascertained exactly when the Company was constituted with a livery, but in 1502 the number of its livery was seventeen, and they ranked as the thirty-seventh out of fifty liveried companies then existing. Among these companies of 1502 were the Mercers with 66 liverymen, the Grocers with 84, the Goldsmiths with 51, the Cutlers with 24, the Armourers with 20, the Innholders with 16, the Masons with 11, the Blacksmiths with 12, the Bakers with 16, the Dyers with 19 and the Plumbers with 12.

It was customary for new liverymen to undergo an initiation ceremony whereby they were dressed in a richly encrusted girdle, and had a hood placed over their heads. In the more recent ceremonies the hood was replaced by a strip of cloth bearing the Company's Arms, which was placed on the new member's shoulders.

To wear the livery was a very expensive business. In 1441 John Scherman, a member of the Coopers' Livery, generously bequeathed his gown, striped with silver, to the Company, and 28s. 6d. was allocated to the Upper Warden in 1540 so that he could pay for his dinner upon taking the oath. Thomas Londysche, Warden in 1523 and responsible for the accounts, wrote, 'The summa totalis of all your payments a lowyd by the holle court, £37. The holle sum of your recaypts ys but £29 19s. 8d. So ys the craft at that accompt clerly in Thomas Londysche dett, £7 0s. 4d.' In 1596 the auditors found defects in the accounts, and fourteen of the ancients of the company were fined a total of £5. Later coopers were able to pay money to avoid the onerous responsibility of office; Wardens and Masters £20, Upper Wardens £12, Under Wardens £6, and Assistants, £5.

A dinner given by the guild in 1539 was costed in the accounts of the Company thus: '3 necks of mutton 10d., a salmon 2s. 8d., 6 rabbits 1s. 4d., 3 geese 2s. 8d., bread and ale 3s., peas 4d., pepper and vinegar 2d., butter 2d., wine 1s. 8d., to the cook for her labour 4d., washing of the clothes 4d., turn-broche 2d.' The fortunes of the Company took, perhaps, a turn for the better when in 1547 they were able to afford sturgeon at ·£1 5s. 0d. It was a recognized practice for the table-napkins to be sewn on to the table-cloths to prevent thefts at these dinners!

To pay for these functions and numerous litigations the coopers relied on payments of quarterage, bequeaths and fines, which were sometimes paid in kind.

Failure to pay dues to the London Company was a very serious offence and could result in a cooper being deprived of his livelihood. In 1503 the Master, accompanied by a Warden, went to the shop of John Thresher, a defaulter, and took away his tools to prevent him working at his trade within the City.

The Company was sufficiently wealthy to afford a ceremonial barge which attended Anne Boleyn from Greenwich to the Tower on her recognition as Queen.

From 1501 the London Coopers Company employed a beadle to 'search, view and gauge all manner of barrels to be made or occupied for ale, beer or sope to be put on sale in London and within two miles compass'. Together with a Warden of the Company he was empowered to seize any cask unmarked or not up to the required standard. Some coopers regarded this as an affront to their dignity, and one, John Gorum, when he was 'raided', called the intruders, '. . . a company of old rascals, and they came down into my yard, whispering, but (God damme), if they were not a parcel of old fellows I would cut off their ears'. For reviling his masters and wardens, Gorum was fined the very punishing sum of £5. The Company Wardens were authorized under an Act of Parliament, 23 Henry VIII, entitled, 'An Act concerning new making of barrels, kilderkins and other vessels,' to ensure that the casks were '. . . marked well and sufficiently, and contained their true contents, rules and measures, and to mark those so viewed with the sign and token of St Anthony's Cross.' Brewers, Soap Merchants, Fish Merchants, Navy Victuallers and others paid for this 'sealing' to be done, as it constituted a qualification similar to a 'British Standards' seal and a guarantee to the customer. The Company sold the privilege of sealing casks to a Mr Chorley in 1554 for £8 a year. In 1569 two sealers were appointed, but by 1592 again one man did the job for which he was paying £16 per year.

In medieval times branding was the mark of good merchandise and bad persons. The Glasgow cooper at this time had to ensure that 8-gallon casks of beef and pork for export were of good timber and tight, for which he was answerable, and if they were discovered to be faulty not only would the cooper be liable to damages but also he would lose his freedom and be banished from the town where he lived. The coopers of Glasgow received their Charter (the Arms are at fig. 66), an 'Act or Letter of Deaconhood' from the Provost, Magistrates and Council of

Glasgow on 27 April 1569, and were recognized as a corporate body with rights of enfranchisement and other privileges. 'Craftismen that are lele trew and of perfite cunnyng and knawlege are putt to povertie and it uter ruyne, throcht wantyng of ordour and non punysing and trying of the faltis of inexpert craftismen . . . wald putt remeid heirto and wald grant to thame ther statutis and articles.'

66. The Glasgow Coopers' Arms.

In 1578 it was decreed that salmon barrels were to hold 12 gallons and herring barrels 9 gallons, though a century later they were changed to 10 and 8¼ respectively.

Coopering in Glasgow could not have been so profitable as in London, for in 1581 an act was passed regarding the fattening of horses during the summer, 'used commonly by people of mean estate, coopers, with the intention of making merchandise of the said horses, for the most part small nags, not serviceable horses'.

It was not until 1693 that the Dean of the Glasgow Guild was authorized to appoint, 'an honest cooper . . . marking with his own mark . . . and call a cooper appointed by a Royal Burgh to try the casks and if they be found sufficient he shall put the public seal . . . the said cooper to have 4/- Scots for each "last" from the maker and each barrel which after such trial be found insufficient be confiscated and disposed of for the use of the poor within the parish where it was made'. Herring casks had to be made of well-seasoned knappell or oak timber free of worm holes, the heads were to be dowelled and the staves to be of ½ in. thickness.

An Act in the reign of Queen Elizabeth I decreed that casks from overseas, converted by the brewers for their own use, must be inspected by the London Coopers Company at the expense of the brewers.

As early as 1531 the coopers could see their independence and monopoly threatened by the growth of the breweries, and they put a bill before Parliament intended to restrict ale-brewers to employing only one cooper and beer-brewers to two. It also stipulated that no brewer was to make casks on his premises. (Beer, involving the use of hop flavouring, was now becoming more popular.) This restriction should have meant that brewers' coopers would have been employed solely in repair and maintenance work as was always the case in Scotland, and new casks would have had to be bought from independent cooperages. At this time breweries were generally very small and numerous, and until the middle of the nineteenth century half of the brewing in this country was done privately. However, the seeds of combination were being sown even in the sixteenth century, for in Chester, innkeepers and ale-sellers petitioned the Mayor and Corporation praying to be protected from the vexations of the brewers who molested them because they brewed their own ale and beer for sale'. By 1591 there were twenty 'great brewhouses' along the Thames from Fleet Street to St Catherine's, and 26,400 barrels of beer were being exported yearly to Ireland and the continent. Despite repeated remonstrances by the Coopers Company, the Act of 1531 was flagrantly disregarded by the Brewers, and costly attempts to put further bills before Parliament were thwarted.

The Elizabethans were very concerned about the tremendous demands being made upon English oak, which was being eaten up by the shipbuilders, the charcoal-burners and builders and furniture-makers as well as by coopers, and because of this laws were passed in 1543 and 1585 prohibiting the export of casks larger than barrels, and making exporters import a corresponding amount of clapboard, or thinly cut timber, for casks. Until this time almost all casks had been made with English oak.

In 1537 the Company placed restrictions upon the number of apprentices a member could employ at any one time. An ordinary member could employ only one, a member of the cloth could employ two, and any member who had been Upper Warden could employ three. The Statute of Artificers decreed that an apprenticeship should last seven years. An order was made in 1547 that every apprentice should give to the craft, in addition to the customary charges, a silver spoon to the value of 6s. 8d. Unfortunately these were all sold from time to time to meet contingencies. Brutal treatment was meted out to disobedient apprentices at this time, and in 1564 the Coopers Company paid, 'for three visors, provided for the punishment of naughty apprentices 3s., and for the whip-stock with whipcord, 6d.' Again in 1578, 'for visor 2s., for rods 2d., for the two men that did whip the two that did offend 1s.'

Despite, or perhaps because of, the harsh treatment they received mobs of apprentices with an abundance of energy were apt to run riot through the streets of London supporting the most undeserving of causes, and politicians were often accused of whipping up the mob. Their brawling was bitter but ephemeral, and uproarious boys were fond of rolling barrels of stones down Dowgate Hill. It seems that today students have taken over this role from the apprentices. Coopers' apprentices were the first among tradesmen to undergo any formal kind of examination. In 1557 seven young men were taken before the London Coopers' Livery and paid 2s. each for their samples and testing, and their proficiency in the craft was accepted following examination by the wardens. Apprentices paid numerous fines to the craft companies upon starting work as journeymen and masters. In Coventry 6s. 8d. was charged for sealing their indentures, and 6s. 8d. again for setting up shop. Craftsmen from the country, who had not served a recognized apprenticeship but had worked honestly for a whole year at their craft, could pay 5s. at the end of the year and another 5s. the next year and then apply to join the craft, but they could never become enfranchised freemen. In 1524 in Coventry, for economic reasons, no limit was put on the number of apprentices a craftsman could employ.

The Newcastle Guild (their Arms are at fig. 67) decreed that, 'No brother must take any more than one apprentice in seven years', and that none should take a Scotsman born to apprentice, nor set any to work, under the penalty of 40s., whereof 26s. 8d. would go to the fraternity and 13s. 4d. to 'Sente Nicholas Kyrkwarke'. By an ordinance of the Corporation of Newcastle (17th of Elizabeth) it was changed to 'one apprentice in four years with the exception of children of the brethren'.

67. The Newcastle Coopers' Arms.

The coopers of Edinburgh, who became part of the Incorporated body known as St Mary's Chapel on 26 August 1489, had an ordinance passed to the effect that

na master nor person of ony of the Craftis tak ony prentis for les terns than sevin yeirs . . . thay sal pay to the altar ane pund of walx the first falt, the second falt twa pundis of walx, the third falt to be pynist be it proved and baillie of the town as affere and allswa quhen ony prentis has completet his termis and is warme out he sall be examaninit be the four men gif he be sufficient or nocht to be a fallow of the Craft, and gif he be worthy to be a fallow he sall pay half a mark to the altar and browke the privilege of the Craft, and gif he be nocht sufficient he sall serf a master quhil he haf livit to be worthy to be a master, and then to be maid freman and fallow . . . and speciale in the withhalding and disobeying in the delivering and paying of the oukly penny to God and to Sanct Jhone and to it reparation of the said altar . . . also the prentis silver at thaw altar, quhilk is 5s.

It was the duty of a Scottish apprentice, together with his master and his master's servants, to turn out in troublous times in defence of 'homes and hearths', under penalty of having all goods confiscated and being banished. The ancient documents and papers of the coopers of

Leith, Edinburgh, were burnt when the English sacked the town in 1544.

While most guilds were making rules for the guidance of apprentices, in Bristol they were drawing the line with regard to wives. Unless a man was ill, away from home or in the debtors' prison, his wife could not buy timber or hoops at the key or back.

As the new Tudor Chartered Companies took over trading from the old foreign companies and trading expanded rapidly, so membership of the Coopers Company of London increased. In 1541 there were 25 members 'of the clothing', 86 members 'out of it' and 13 Dutchmen. By 1547 the numbers had increased to 40 of the livery, 75 ordinary members, 57 Dutchmen, 13 free denizens and 9 foreigners, free journeymen, 192 in all. By 1553 the numbers had grown to 267. London itself grew in population from 60,000 in 1540 to 300,000 in 1640. There were a considerable number of Dutchmen, Huguenots, escaping the atrocities perpetrated on the Continent, and they must have caused a little friction, for in 1524 an Act was passed empowering one substantial stranger to be responsible to see that all of them complied with the rulings of the Company. Should they refuse to be searched by Company Officers they were to be debarred from trading.

Newcastle coopers were forbidden to employ Dutchmen.

The act of 1531 had fixed the price at which coopers could sell new casks, but within a decade or so the rising cost of living, a familar phrase, caused protests from coopers suffering hardship. It was therefore decreed in an Act (8 Elizabeth) of 1565 that Mayors in towns, and Justices of the Peace in country districts, could fix higher prices, and so alleviate any distress.

Translations, or transferences from one company to another, occurred in 1545 when a skinner became a cooper and in the following year a cooper became a goldsmith. In 1559 a cooper became a clothworker and in 1581 three goldsmiths became coopers. In these times this would be done for trading purposes, but later, when membership of the companies was bought in order to acquire status, it was necessary if a man aspired to high office in City affairs.

'Any work for Johnny Cooper?' was a familiar cry through the streets of London during Tudor times and in following centuries, despite the efforts of the Company to stop the hawking for work. A ruling of 1561 made hawking an offence and informers were paid to track them down.

The Companies of the City were charged with fitting out troops and ships for the king's wars. The accounts of the Coopers Company for 1537 read,

Provided and set forth four men towards the king's wars in the North Country, horse, bows and daggers. Gave two of the horses to three of the men and sold the third; the fourth man deserted with his horse, saddle and all. £10. . . . 1542, two more men. . . . 1544, six men (two bowmen and four bill-men). . . . 1559, making forth two soldiers to sea, £1 2s. 2d. . . . 1564, five to Newhaven £9 4s. 7d. . . . 1566, one soldier to Ireland £2 6s. 5d. . . . 1569, twelve soldiers to the North £50. . . . 1577, 25 soldiers furnished £18 18s. 0½d. . . . 1579, five soldiers and the provision of furniture for the soldiers, £6 13s. 1d. . . . 1580, thirty-eight soldiers to the Queen's ships. . . . 1585, eight soldiers with 17 days at 8d. a day. . . . 1586, 262 pounds of gunpowder at ten pence a pound. Transporting 200 soldiers to the Low Countries. . . . 1587, three barrels of gunpowder sold to the Mynion, one of the ships set forth by the City, received £9 15s. 0d. . . . Towards setting out twenty sail, £1 10s. 0d. . . . Towards training 1,000 soldiers, 7s. 6d. . . . 1591, paid and received for setting out ships £47. . . .

This must have been quite a drain on the Company. The inventory of Company property for 1570 included bills, 32 swords, 29 daggers, vizards, whips, 19 calivers, 15 pikes with armings of fustian, fringed bows, drum and sticks, 13 corslets, 19 flax and touchboxes, 17 morions and 31 girdles for swords—the necessary appendages of a sixteenth-century company.

With industrial regulations passing into the hands of the State and being organized on a national basis the coopers needed to put bills through parliament instead of before the Lord Mayor at Guildhall, as they had done previously. These bills proved to be terribly expensive. In 1566 we read:

Charges for repealing former statutes concerning beer, ale and soap vessels, £20 2s. 7d. . . . 1588, Expenses in obtaining an Act of Parliament for gauging foreign vessels, £30 13s. 2d. . . . 1592, Paid for a bill preferred to Parliament against the Brewers for keeping above two coopers in their houses against the statute 23 Hen. VIII, £5 4s. 2d. . . . 1597, Towards two bills one of which passed but was afterwards put back, including £1 13s. 4d. . . . ipocrass for the Lords, £47 6s. 7d.

On top of this were the hidden costs. 'Paid for a little barrel of muscadine of three gallons and a pottle given to Master North, Clerk of the Parliament, dwelling in Wood Street, 2s. 10d., a bottle to the serjeant's servant as reward, 8d., for a weker bottle given to the serjeant, 2d., to the serjeant that kept the door, 8d.' is entered in the accounts of the Coopers Company. But this is small stuff when compared to the entry of 1562, 'Paid as in reward to the Speaker, one

61. Anglo-Saxon drinking stoups

62. The Marlborough Vat

63. One of two butts excavated from Sutton Hoo
(reconstructed)

64. The wine trade

65. Household vessels

66. The fruit bowl; in the Glastonbury Iron-Age tradition

67. The washing tub

68. The wooden bucket

69. A seventeenth-century well bucket

70. An old Guild Hall

71. Sixteenth-century washer women

72. Coopers' marks, 1420

73. The London Company of Coopers' Arms

74. An eighteenth-century truck, convenient for casks

75. Coopered vessels used in wine-making in the early
sixteenth century

runlet with ten gallons of sack, 16s. 6d.' Bribery must have been re-
warding, for in 1533 the Speaker received an even bigger one, a pipe
of Gascony Wine worth £3 6s. 8d. The Company paid £2 3s. 4d. for a
half-butt of malmsey given to the Lord Chancellor in 1533. Two years
later he was the recipient of a hogshead of wine, as was the Lord
Mayor, all in all, £2 3s. 4d. The Lord Chief Justice was not above
accepting 20 gallons of sack (sherry) costing £1 3s. 4d. in 1561, although
a special reference is made to the effect that it was given by consent.
Two hogsheads of wine for the Lord Mayor cost the Company £5 15s. 0d.
in 1566. 'In thankfulness for his favour to the Company in his opposi-
tion in Parliament to the Vintners', the Lord Mayor, Bolton received

68. Tankard from sixteenth-century Swedish ship Vasa.

a hogshead of wine in 1667. So much for the scruples and integrity of
the political leaders of the day. However, it is possible that one of
these leaders learnt in no uncertain terms what was thought of him,
for Cooper Thomas Hynde was fined the nominal sum of one shilling
in 1540 for 'words that he spoke in my Lord Chancellor's House'.
Despite these drains upon their resources the Company was still able
to lend the Queen £50 in 1557 and £80 in 1598, the latter being repaid
in 1599. They lent the King £60 in 1604; repaid in 1606.

Master Maycotts, the clerk who audited the books, was paid a goodly
sum of money for his trouble, plus the inevitable 'perk' in the form of
a bottle of muscadyll.

Some of the richer Livery Companies ran schools and almshouses,
and the Coopers Company was no exception. A grammar school, together with almshouses for fourteen poor distressed persons of the

Company, was founded at Ratcliff in the Port of Stepney in 1538 by Nicholas Gibson, a grocer, who left them to his wife. She married Sir Anthony Knyvett, who surrendered the property to the Company in 1552. Schoolhouse Lane took its name from this school. The charity was increased during the times of the Tudors and Stuarts by the benefactions of Henry Cloker in 1573, and Toby Wood in 1611.

Cooper-made tankards were still in demand in these days, perhaps not as cleverly made as the wonderful little *situlae* of the Anglo-Saxons, but rather similar to the one drawn in fig. 68, retrieved from the sixteenth-century Swedish ship Vasa. In 1540 Cooper John Herth paid the Company a fine of 2s. 9d. for selling four 'evil-made' tankards. When Sir Francis Drake dropped anchor in Port St Julian, South America, on his epic world journey, he came across the gibbet upon which, fifty-seven years earlier, Magellan had hung mutineers on his famous voyage. The cooper of the *Pelican* is said to have cut sections of this gibbet for staves with which to make tankards, 'for such of the company who would drink from them'. Drake deliberately destroyed thousands of barrels and staves during his daring raid on Cadiz when he 'singed the King of Spain's beard'. When at last the Armada sailed in 1588 its provisions were contained in hastily found or newly made casks, many of which were quickly 'bodged', old, worm-eaten or of rotting wood, or else of new unseasoned 'green' wood, which shrank and warped, causing their contents to leak and spoil. Historians have emphasized the effects of the fireships off Gravelines and the English culverines and half-culverines, but with their provisions deteriorating in the holds the Spaniards were already demoralized, and it can be said that the battle against the Armada was at least half won when the Spanish barrels went up in flames in the Cadiz raid. One can imagine the plight of the Spaniards from the numerous letters sent to our own Commissioners for Victualling, H.M. Navy, from ships at sea, complaining of faulty casks and leakages due to worm holes, bad joints or rotten wood. Sometimes a complaint from a ship would be that the beer, or water, was stinking and unfit to drink, and very occasionally this sort of letter, sent by Captain Brown of the *Feversham* off Antigua, on 24 June. 1722, 'Sir, . . . the men have been put on short rations, (four days food, water and beer to last six) . . . the meat has decayed very fast, eat out so much by the salt, that it is hardly sufficient to support the sailors. . . . neither will the peas break after boiling them for eight hours, they are served to the men as hard as shot . . . many are very ill and we are scarce able to subsist'. If this sort of thing could

69. Coopers at work in Germany, 1586.

happen in a comparatively well-organized navy over a century later, what must it have been like with the Spanish Armada'? Deliberately reduced and hurriedly scraped together, the casks were unlikely to have passed the scrutiny of a Coopers' Company Beadle, or the Master

Cooper of a Royal Navy Victualling Yard. Of course there is another side to the story in that many of the claims for lost wine were, no doubt, fictitious and fraudulent, and many of the holes in the casks were of human origin. A common trick, rife up to this day, was to bore two very small holes into a cask, small enough to be plugged by a piece of twig and difficult to detect, to blow through one and catch the wine pouring out of the other in a bottle. This was called, 'sucking the monkey'.

Fig. 69 shows coopers at work in a German Cooperage, and the costumes worn give the clue to the period. The illustration is taken from The Cooper (der Butner) from the Sachs-Amman Staendebuch of 1568. The tool being used by the cooper in the background to stretch the wooden hoops over the cask is one still used by wine coopers on the continent, and called the traitoire. The wash-tub (fig. 70) was used

70. The wash tub.

more for medicinal purposes than with any conception of hygiene or comfortable living. We have good reason to call our ancestors, 'the great unwashed'.

Pl. 75 shows a variety of cooper-made vessels, all with wooden hoops, being used for wine-making. It is from a print in the British Museum from an early sixteenth-century Flemish calendar. The cooper with the adze is fitting a wooden bung, wrapped in sacking, into the bung hole.

In a Flemish calendar for the year 1500 (*pl. 76*), a woman is portrayed sitting in a coopered barrel that has been made into an armchair. Throughout history casks and tubs have been modified to provide furniture, particularly in the poorer homes. However, as these vessels are held together by the friction of the hoops against the staves, when they are kept in a dry atmosphere they tend to shrink, the hoops fall off, and they will drop apart unless they are coopered and tightened again when the wood is thoroughly dried out. *Pls. 77* and *78* show coopered vessels which have been adopted for use in the home, and anyone having sat in one of the armchairs or a similar one will vouch for the fact that they are very comfortable indeed.

Pieter Bruegel's famous work, 'Children's Games', painted in 1560, shows a number of children playing with casks. Child psychologists today place great emphasis on the extent to which children learn through play. What lessons have been learnt through the centuries from old barrels?

CHAPTER TWELVE

The Stuart Period

Following in the wake of discoveries, world trade expanded rapidly in the Stuart period, and consequently this period saw a very noticeable growth in the realm of coopering. Wine was being imported in considerable quantities, and in fact, prior to 1626, the tonnage of a ship was based on the carrying capacity of ships engaged in the Bordeaux Wine Trade. The unit was a tun of wine in two butts, equalling 252 gallons, and occupying 60 cu. ft. After 1626 it was estimated empirically as 207 old, equalling 176 new, and only in modern times has it become possible to calculate exact tonnage.

Some coopers did a certain amount of business importing wines, to which the Vintners Company objected. In the legal feud which followed the coopers met with success in 1641 and again in 1667 (no doubt helped considerably by the bribed Mayor, Bolton), and in 1693 and 1697 they petitioned the government against raising the import duties on wines from Spain and Portugal, duties which had already reduced the sale of their wines by half. The coopers would appear to have had a double interest here, for wine casks were at this time being made in this country with Memel oak from the Baltic, and shipped to Spain and Portugal, but at the turn of the century, presumably to exploit the cheaper Portuguese labour and to rationalize the trading, English coopers went to Portugal and taught the Portuguese how to make casks. In a letter of 1704, Thomas Woodman, a wine-importer, wrote from Portugal, 'Ye English cupers are a drunken lot, but ye natives now know how to make casks . . . ye heat is so great that breathing is difficult . . . the cupers are here and at work.' Some 200 years later a Portuguese cooperage was turning out 25,000 casks a year by machinery. The Methuen Treaty of 1703 reduced the duty on port wine so that it became a very popular drink. It was said that the English vessels would 'barter a nigger for a pipe'.

The New England settlers soon found that they could add to their incomes appreciably by felling the American White Oaks and converting them into barrel staves in the forests surrounding their coastal settlements. Many learnt from the coopers who had emigrated how to make casks, and during the long winter evenings, pipes, barrels, tubs, pails and churns were produced in large numbers. They supplied the casks for West Indian rum, being shipped to Bristol in the notorious 'Triangular trade', although thousands of cask staves were made in Bristol and sent across the Atlantic. From Virginia and the more Southern states planters were constantly writing to their agents in England asking them to procure skilled coopers, and many went as indentured servants, being free to work at their trade after a few years of bound coopering for a planter. However, white craftsmen in the South soon found themselves working in competition with slaves, and most who could save a small amount of capital became landowners and planters themselves.

A tremendous variety of commodities was now being shipped by cask: water, beer and ale, wines, rum and other spirits, oils, fish of all kinds, sugar, syrup, apples, cider, tobacco, green ginger, shoes, crockery, nails, cork, gunpowder, lead, paint, grease, seeds, pearl-barley, meats, butter, vinegar, putty, money and a thousand other types of goods, and as the amount of trade increased so coopers were able to specialize more and more, and the branches of the trade, as outlined in Chapter 2, became more clearly defined.

Today packages are made to contain specific quantities or weights by mathematical calculation. The rather quaint sizes of casks owe their origins to far more diverse and interacting intentions. The availability of timber, coopering ability, tradition, local pride, petty arbitrary decisions and downright cussedness all played their part in determining cask sizes, but despite this they came to be accepted as official units of measurement. Kings and governments tried to standardize units. In 1423 we had the 'hogges hede' fixed at 63 old wine gallons, that is 52½ gallons. Richard III fixed wine barrels at 31½ gallons. Henry VI stipulated 30-gallon barrels for eels, which Edward IV changed to 42 gallons to include salmon and spruce. George III made it 38 wine gallons. Henry VIII fixed ale barrels at 32 gallons, country ale at 34, and beer at 36; vinegar was to be in 34-gallon barrels. Oil, spirits, tar and pork were fixed at 36 gallons. Charles II decreed that barrels of plates, crockery, must hold 300 pounds. George III fixed apple barrels at 24 gallons, and gunpowder casks at 100 pounds. Casks and coopers were laws unto themselves, and irrespective of how irrational these sizes became during the course of time, they remained an inviolable 'mistery' to confuse the layman.

A common sight in London during the fifteenth, sixteenth and seventeenth centuries was the water-carrier, and even in the eighteenth century Londoners bought pailfuls of water at their doors for a penny, from watermen carrying churns and calling, 'Fresh and fair, New River water!' (fig. 71).

Early Tudor and Stuart fire-fighting equipment consisted of a cask fitted on a cart and drawn by a horse or by men (fig. 72).

John Amos Comenius, a Czechoslovakian, writing in 1659 a 'Nomenclature of the Chief Things, and Man's Employment in the World', 'Orbis Sensualium Pictus', said of the cooper (fig. 73),

The Cooper (1) having an apron (2) tied about him, maketh hoops (3) of hazel rods upon a cutting block (4) with a spokeshave (5) and lags (6) of timber. Of lags he maketh hogsheads (7) and pipes (8) with two heads, and tubs (9) soes (10) flaskets (11) buckets (12) with one bottom, then he bindeth them with hoops (13) which he tyeth fast with small twigs (14) by means of a cramp-iron (15) and he fitteth them on with a mallet (16) and a driver (17).

It was evidently the hoops which caught his interest.

In some parts of the country, notably Bristol, the trade of coopering was shared by two tradesmen, the cooper and the hooper. The cooper made the cask and heads while the hooper made the hoops, fitted the heads into position and drove the hoops home. Piecework wages were shared equally. The Hoopers Company of Bristol dates from 1504, and among their forty-five rules was one which stated that every hoop brought into Bristol had to be examined to ensure that it was sound, and was then stamped C.B., Civitus Bristoliensis.

The cutting of hazel branches and the making of fences, baskets, fish-traps and hoops have been specialist woodland trades, preceding that of the cooper. Hoop-making in Sussex, the Midlands and Furness grew with the growth of coopering, and an export trade with Jamaica developed about this time in sugar-barrel hoops, ending early this century. Hazel branches were cut and split with an adze, trimmed with a draw knife, as in the illustration, where it is called a spoke-shave, and coiled on a 'horse' or a frame of upright pegs, after having been soaked to make them pliable. Coopers would make them to size by notching the overlapping ends and binding or nailing them. Hoop-makers also made standard-size hoops for dry work, in huge quantities, nailing them together within an ash measuring hoop, similar to the truss hoop used for bending staves (see Part 1, Chapter 5). One man would make between 400 and 500 hoops a day. Trade diminished with the decline

71. The water carrier.

72. The fire cart.

73. Czech coopers at work, 1659.

74. Coopers at work in Amsterdam, 1694.

in coopering in the nineteenth century, and with cheap rolled steel hoops coming on to the market, so that although in 1949 it was still being carried on, today it is practically extinct.

Describing coopering in another way, Christof Wazel of Regensburg, Germany, wrote in 1698, 'The cross preserves that which would otherwise fall to pieces. The band (hoop), the precious word by God imparted for the quiet life of devotion, is that which must enclose the noble fluid of the soul securely in the heart. If it lacks, the power will flow away and man remain an empty cask.' Large casks would often have a cross-piece of wood fitted on to the head after the cask had been tightened, to give additional support. In Luiken's engraving of the cooper (fig. 74) he is using an iron driver and hitting it with a mallet, in order to tighten the hoop on the cask. An iron driver of that type is at *pl. 79*, and a hoop driver, used mostly for dry work until the nineteenth century, is at fig. 75. The wooden stock driver (see Chapter 5) was already in use at this time. In the eighteenth-century illustrations of coopering by Forgeroux, a French wine cooper is pictured using a mallet on a tapered block of wood, while in thirteenth-century Italy two mallets were used, one being held on to the hoop and being struck by the other.

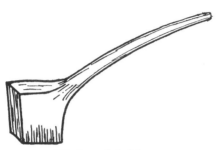

75. A metal driver.

During the seventeenth century the companies of London suffered considerable interference in their affairs by the Stuart Kings, who saw in the companies an easy means of extorting money. The Stuart Kings nominated their own candidates for all key posts. One can imagine the quandary of the coopers when in 1673 both the King and the Lord Mayor wrote letters supporting different candidates applying for the post of clerk. Sackings and resignations were frequent, and the feud came to a head when James II suspended the charters of the companies in 1685. William and Mary, upon their accession, restored the City of London to its ancient rights and privileges, but by then the medieval system of trading was beginning to give way to ideas of *laissez-faire*, and the technical nature of the companies with regard to their trades began to take secondary importance to the social and charitable side, and in line with the ethics of the day membership, involving freedom of the City, became more and more the prerogative of the wealthy.

The Coopers Company raised £350 in 1643 towards £50,000 raised by the companies for the Parliamentarians, and in 1664 raised £600 towards a loan to the King; they also subscribed, rather reluctantly, towards building a frigate. The Company had contributed £140 towards a plantation in Ireland, later called the Irish Society, and established in order to colonize the country. This was in 1609, but by 1612 they asked leave to discontinue payments, and forfeited all rights. To make these huge payments the Company sold its plate and spoons.

In 1632 the Company was assessed at £7 towards the City's fine of £1,000 for the murder of Dr Lambe. The younger warden paid this himself, 'for love of the Company, and in return for not being chosen younger warden again'. Presumably he wanted to escape the onerous and costly duties associated with the work of a London Company Official.

The Great Fire devoured the Company's Hall in 1666, together with a lot of houses owned by the coopers for which they collected rents. Most of the treasures, books and registers were taken to the house of the Upper Warden and saved. In 1668 the coopers began the construction of another hall, and instituted compulsory subscriptions; £1,078 17s. 5d. in 1668, £2,029 12s. in 1669, £1,082 2s. in 1670, and £998 15s. in 1671, when the Hall was completed at a cost of £5,189 6s. 5d., a tremendous sum of money for those times. Whether the expunging of five liverymen in 1672 because of poverty resulted from this sacrifice is not known; however, the Coopers still put on a brave and proud face, for in 1663 they had collected £154 10s. towards a barge which they used for the Lord Mayor's celebrations and in 1687 were employing a bargemaster, a mate and fourteen watermen.

During the plague in 1665, Francis Hall, a pluralist with the living at the local church of St Michaels, Bassishaw, left London for the safety of the country, and his other living at Market Deeping. On his return in 1670 he demanded back-payment of tithes, which the coopers regarded as monstrous, and there was 'bad blood' between the Church and the Company until 1675 when the coopers agreed to let the gallery of their hall to the incumbent for Sunday meetings at a rent of £20 per annum.

The sealing of casks brought in considerable revenue for the London Company during the sixteenth century. Around the middle of the century it was yielding £137 per annum, of which the Company received £50.

Informers were still being paid in 1620, and soap casks were publicly burnt in 1685, while as late as 1693 a merchant was prosecuted for 'ingrossing' with casks. A regulation which would realize a considerable sum of money today came into force in 1667, whereby apprentices appearing for registration were fined 6d. if they had extra long hair. It has been said that the apprentice during these times was in no better situation than the fourteenth-century serf. Many trades could be learnt well within the seven years of bound apprenticeship, and for most of this time he constituted cheap labour. If he ran away he was cried and forcibly brought back, often ill if not brutally treated as an indoor servant, with a poor diet and obliged to sleep in the workshop. This, no doubt, applied to many a young cooper's apprentice. In the summer they were prominent in their blue cloaks with breeches and stockings of white broadcloth, and in winter, long blue gowns. They wore flat caps, for which they were often derided, but worked in tall square hats which had shelves fitted to the insides, so that, for coopers at least, the saying, 'Keep it under your hat' must have meant something.

An apprenticeship bond made out in Edinburgh in 1703 stated that a prentice and servant, failing him by decease (of the master) to be bound to his relict if he shall have any, she keeping sufficient journeymen for his instruction in the airt and trade of coupercraft . . . six years binds himself faithfully, dutifully and honestly to attend to he said master's service night and day, holyday and workday, in all things lawful and honest and shall not absent himself under penalty of two days service for each day's absence, and that he communicates to his master anything that he sees or hears to the prejudice of his master's goods or good name, under penalty of 2d. for every 1d. loss . . . He must abstain from cairding, dyceing, drinking, swearing, nightwaking and debauchering and other idle exercise that may divert him from his master's service, and if he commit the filthie crimes of fornication or adulterie at any time before the expiry of the said six years for three years thereafter as if he were in new bond again . . . to be given clothing due to his rank, be taught and instructed by able and qualified master who shall dine and entertain him at bed and board decently and honestly . . . binded by £40.

In the Minute Book of the Aberdeen Coopers of 1682 is a paragraph: 'Apprentices for meat and fee to work one year after the five (no fewer); failure to do so . . . to lose the benefit of his prentisship and be classed as an extranean'. So the length of apprenticeship was already being reduced. It was further ordained in Aberdeen that at the end of an apprenticeship there would be a test of workmanship, called an essay. The cooper had to make, 'ane salmond salt for holding four barrels of salmond, or ane three boll salt for brewing; one firlot and peck, ane salmond barrel conforming to bind and measure of Aberdeen, the goadges made for that effect to be given to hem be the deacon and masters'. The masters were to examine the work done without speaking to each other, and declare their voices to the clerk.

An Aberdeen apprenticeship was made valuable by a ruling in 1747 that no coopers were to be employed unless they had served their apprenticeship in the town, and in the preamble to this were the proud words, 'as the coupers of Aberdeen have been so long famous for the best work all over the kingdom, so they could not be so much answerable for a journeyman's work who had not been bred with some of themselves'. The arms are at fig. 76.

76. The Aberdeen Wrights and Coopers' Arms.

Every week the coopers of Aberdeen, who had joined with the wrights (all other woodworkers) into a guild, one of seven in the city and known as the Wrights and Coopers, obtaining their 'seals of cause' in 1532, used to take their goods to the Market Cross where they held a Timmer Market. They became a powerful guild in Aberdeen, importing their own timber and ensuring their monopoly. In 1696 they were granted arms comprising a shield with four squares and in each a tool, two wright's tools and two cooper's, and they took it in turn year about to appoint a master.

The coopers of Edinburgh were not so prosperous about this time, being £100 in arrears with payments due to the Chapel of St Mary's, and making the excuse that their 'box was very low' (the treasurer was called the boxmaster incidentally). They might not have been so poor if the

77. Seventeenth-century coopers at work.

coopers of Leith had been more forthcoming in their payments, but these people were complaining about the fact that they had to waste time and money waiting for a cooper to come from the Royal burgh of Edinburgh to gauge and mark their casks at the quay as satisfactory for export, and they resented this. They could not have their own gauger as they were not a Royal burgh. They had other grievances. Certain brewers were employing unfreemen, and their 'liberty was prejudiced by the frequent concourse of strangers who daily repair to Leith with barrels and other commodities belonging to the trade without paying any of the public burden and taxation borne by the craft'. They considered themselves wronged by the shoremaster who exacted dues for 'timber, skowes, girrds and knappels as if they were strangers, thus hindering them from working'. Outside of Leith their coopers had been threatened with 'mischief, bluid and murther', and a riot was committed by a George Johnston upon one of their freemen 'while has beine hard with so mutch greif of hart before the barron baylzie which jars if not prevented will undoubtedly end in more bluid and mischief'.

Coopers were described by Holme in 1688 thus, '. . . in his waist-coat and cap, breeches and hose russet, with an adze lifted up in his right hand and a driver in his left, trussing up a barrel with fire out of the top of it'. The reference to his tools and work would equally well fit a cooper of the twentieth century.

J. J. van Vliet's painting of coopers at work is shown in fig. 77. Regulations were passed in 1672 requiring all barrels and kilderkins to have three wooden hoops on the chime and three at the booge, as can be seen in the painting.

When Otto von Guericke first experimented with an air pump around 1650 it was natural that he should choose a barrel as the vessel in which to create a vacuum. The pressure it had to take would have been 14.7 lb. per square inch; if a cask can withstand 2 lb. it will hold water, and in the United States in the twentieth century dry-tight casks were tested at 5 lb. Extra stout brewers' casks with extra hoops on the pitch could withstand over 30 lb. the head being the most vulnerable part and tending to blow out. *Pl* 80 shows von Guericke's first experiment.

76. The barrel chair, 1500

77. The barrel chair

78. Coopered furniture

79. A metal driver

80. Creating a vacuum, 1669 (von Guericke's first air pump)

81. The Heidelberg Tun

82. Broad Quay, Bristol, eighteenth century

83. A smugglers' Inn

84. Coopers at work, eighteenth century

85. King Alexander's submarine—the inevitable barrel

86. The Coopers' Hall, Bristol

87. The last issue of grog. The end of another great tradition involving the cooper

88, 89. The development of casks, drays and artistry over some
hundreds of years

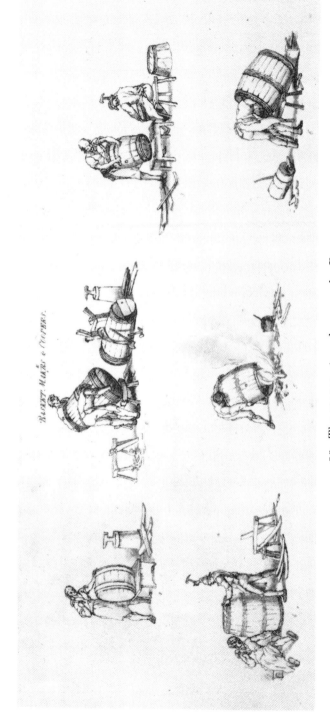

90. The cooper at work as seen by Pyne

CHAPTER THIRTEEN

The Eighteenth Century

'A tradesman may,' wrote Defoe, 'on occasion, keep company with a gentleman.' He was voicing the sentiments of the day whereby the tradesman was becoming a genuinely respected figure in society as a whole. That great lower-middle class of respectable people, so reviled by popularity-seeking writers as hypocrites, but who somehow consolidated those things in our society which were worth preserving and formed the backbone of our democracy and our economy, was coming into its own.

In many cases a tavern became the recognized rendezvous for men of a particular trade, and so we had, among others, 'The Coopers' Arms', where masters and men discussed employment, pay and grievances generally, while wages were often paid there, in the public bar, no doubt to the immense pleasure and satisfaction of the landlord.

Casks had for long been so commonplace that they were often the subject of sayings. A 'tub-thumper' was the equivalent of a soap-box orator, and if he told a 'tale of a tub', people might realize that it was a cock-and-bull story. When a small ship was threatened by a whale it would be necessary to create a diversion by throwing a tub overboard, and so came the old, now archaic saying, 'throw a tub to a whale.'

Up to the middle of this century the cask was still used as a means of punishment. With one head removed and a hole cut into the other through which a man could put his head, and with two holes in the staves for his hands to go through, it was a form of humiliation for a drunkard or a scold to parade through the streets dressed in such a barrel (fig. 78).

Many of the old inns around our coasts bear witness to the considerable traffic in wines and spirits which were smuggled ashore in all manner of disguises to evade the iniquitous customs officers. Smuggling was never considered to be a great wrong, as taxes and duties were crudely assessed and bribery was rife. One early way of deciding how much ought to be paid in duty was for the gauger, or tax-collector,

78. The drunkard's cloak.

to sit in his leather breeches in a pool of beer for thirty minutes; if he stuck, it was strong and taxed at 2s. a barrel, otherwise only 6d. would have to be paid. Excise duties were also assessed haphazardly and arbitrarily by tasters and surveyors using 'rule of thumb' methods always allowing a hogshead before and behind the mast; the good wine was carried behind the mast for safety. One of the most picturesque of inns, overlooking three quiet coves with hidden rooms and still possessing a few treasured little brandy casks dating back to this period, is shown at *pl. 83*. The oval casks, used as tables, are called barricoes, and made so that they would not roll and endanger the boats; they were used in lifeboats until after the Great War and would certainly have been used by smugglers.

A barrel could be a very useful article in a sailing ship which found itself being chased by a pirate, or an enemy, during the frequent wars. Under cover of darkness the crew would fix a light to a cask, lower it into the sea and set it adrift, then with all lights extinguished the ship would alter course, leaving the decoy to be followed.

The cost of cooperage in the Navy during this period must have been very considerable, as they insisted upon having iron-bound casks for watering their ships. In 1764 hoop iron was costing between £23 and £24 a ton. A statement of costs issued by the Cooperage Office of the Victualling Board for 1805, when coke-smelting must have made iron somewhat less costly, gives the cost of old iron hoops as 3d. each, and new iron hoops as 10d. each, whereas wooden hoops were 3s. 9d., and smaller ones 2s. 6d. per 'hundred of six score'. This was called a long hundred, and is derived from the time of Danelaw, when counting was always in multiples of six. A new barrel cost 3s. 3d., but if it were to be bound with iron hoops these alone would cost 5s. Consequently it was the custom, when taking stock, to count the iron hoops on the casks, for the inventory. The wreck of the *Hind* on the rocks off Jersey in 1722 gave up seventeen casks and eighty iron hoops, it was reported. For years a widow sought payment for 400 iron hoops deposited at a naval stores by her late husband, and this would obviously have realized a good sum of money.

Around the middle of the century coopers were fitting two narrow hoops on the chime (the end) of the casks, known as square and chime hoops. Isaac Cotterell, a master cooper of Bristol, writing in 1768, said that the wide chime hoop, as it was used on all brewers' casks from then on, had been invented by a Captain David Duncombe, and known as a 'Worm Tub Chime Hoop'. The chime is the most vulnerable part of the cask, because if it suffers a blow here it tends to crack across the stave to the groove, so that a wide strong hoop gives considerable protection.

To be a cooper in the Victualling Yards of the Navy in these days was a sought-after job; so much so that in 1715 the Admiralty received two letters of recommendation for a certain Sam Mallbroke, neither of which stated whether or not he could make a cask, but in the ethics of the day stressed that he was a freeman, married to a free baron (a term used commonly in medieval times to describe the aldermanic aristocracy) of the town of Chatham, that there were 'several relations who desire of how to assist him', and that to employ him would oblige the writers. The Admiralty wrote to the Master Cooper of Chatham agreeing to Sam being employed, and back came the reply, '. . . thanks for your favour . . . I will be very tender of giving you any trouble of like nature. This was occasioned by the importunities of some people who are always craving, and think I can never do enough for them'.

A painting of the English School, of Broad Quay, Bristol, shows the predominance of coopered vessels (*pl. 82*); many were carried on low skids with small, 6 in., solid metal wheels, pulled by one horse (*pl. 74*).

In 1684 the Navy Victuallers refused to allow their casks to be gauged and marked by the Coopers Company, who made many complaints against the Commissioners of Admiralty, the last in 1703, without success. By 1729 there was only one sealer employed by the coopers. His services were needed even less when the soapmakers decided that they did not want their casks to be sealed; and in 1733 a complaint by the coopers was rejected. The brewers, who had regarded the seal as a mark of quality, refused to undertake to pay the costs after 1775, so the sealing of casks came to an end.

Gin had had been encouraged in order to supplant French brandy imports, consume surplus grain and create employment, but this did not help the coopers when it sold at the expense of beer. Although gin was kept in casks, where it would 'mellow', or colour if the cask had previously held sherry, modern rectification techniques have replaced the necessity for it to mature in the cask, and no coopers are now employed in the gin industry.

Breweries were becoming very large towards the end of the century. The rivalry of the gin-distillers was virtually ended with the tax of 1751. Dr Johnson had said, when involved in the selling of Thrale's Brewery to Barclay, 'Sir, we are not here to sell a parcel of boilers and vats, but the potentiality of growing rich beyond the dreams of avarice.' The Barclays were called before the Coopers Company in 1792 and again in 1797 regarding the making of casks on their premises. On the first occasion £10 was placed in the poor box, and a promise was made to destroy all truss hoops (thick ash hoops used in the firing or bending of casks). The penalty imposed upon brewers who made their own casks in defiance of City ordinances was approximately the cost of a barrel of beer for each offence.

Up to the eighteenth century the Company had been run by coopers, and technical knowledge was essential, but by now a great many people, particularly Jewish, in order to acquire status, respectability and freemanship with City enfranchisement, bought their way into the old companies. They began to monopolize the higher livery, and in fact it became so expensive to attend Guildhall banquets and ceremonials that few master coopers could afford it. Robert Willimot, a Liveryman Cooper, in 1743 became the first Lord Mayor of London to be appointed outside the twelve senior companies, and later in 1767 Sir James Esdaile, of the Coopers Company, became the second Lord Mayor from the Company.

The costs to an apprentice coming out of his time were very considerable. Before he could regard himself as a London journeyman cooper he had to pay a series of fines; 3 gallons for his footing, another for each piece of work done for the first time, and an extra gallon for every different sort of timber used. Even with beer at 1s. 2d. a gallon his fines would exceed his week's pay of about 15s. 9d. In 1787 the coopers got together in a society, continuing the fines in order to get financially established, but owing to a defaulting treasurer the society collapsed. In 1795 another society was established for the relief of old men in the trade, and the fines were reduced to 2 gallons of beer. Fines were discontinued completely upon the establishing of societies in the early 1820s. There were four in London, the Philanthropic Society of London, the Amalgamated Society of London, the United Society of London, and the Hand in Hand Society of Coopers, established in 1824. These Friendly Societies were springing up all over the country at this time with the need for insurance and security in a rapidly changing society, encouraged by the prevailing ideas of self-help in an 'every man for himself' system, and tradesmen, embittered by the economic thinkers with their 'iron law of wages', flocked to join, and displayed their membership certificates proudly framed over their mantelpieces.

Although 'proof work' was presented and personal marks were allocated as late as 1740, the Coopers Company was more concerned with administering the charities and the formalities of an ancient livery company. However, a trade examination was still held up until the last cooper passed out in the 1960s, with a warden, a liveryman and a representative of the firm of the cooper's apprentice, all taking part in the examination to ensure that the apprentice could make a cask satisfactorily.

Similarly the old companies of other cities were changing with the times or becoming defunct as their usefulness came to an end. Tradition and love of ceremony played their part. The coopers and joiners were one of twelve companies of Gloucester which attended upon the Mayor in 1779. The coopers were the last trade company to survive in Hull. They had a hall in Hailes Entry, High Street, with the Arms of the King and the coopers proudly displayed above, and the motto, 'Fear God, honour the King and love the Brethren'. Annually they took part in a procession, exhibiting their plate which was of considerable value. Those companies which tried to preserve their ancient customs found themselves up against laws passed in the spirit of the age. A mandamus was taken out by a Messrs Coates against the Coopers' Company of Newcastle in 1797, after they had tried to enforce customary restrictions on apprentices and their numbers, and it was determined that corporations had no right to make by-laws 'in restraint of trade'.

In 1755 a cooper and freeman of London, William Godfrey, was seized by a press gang in his house. Such was his status that after a court case the midshipman in charge of the gang was fined £5 and jailed for one year.

A cooperage of this period is shown at *pl. 84.*

It was during the American War of Independence that a colonial cooper, David Bushnell, built what was claimed to be the world's first submarine, the *Turtle,* in reality a very large wooden cask, in the coopers' shop of Joseph Borden at Bordentown, New York. To cause it to submerge jettisonable ballast was fitted to the outside, and the propeller was turned by hand from inside the submarine. Unfortunately it had no periscope, and it was impossible after having travelled for any distance submerged to know one's exact whereabouts without actually coming to the surface, which defeated its object. The colonial coopers were quite ingenious, but the idea had already been circulated in the *Romance of Alexander,* written in 1340 in Flanders, and at *pl. 85* is the drawing of King Alexander's submarine, unmistakably a barrel. A floating mine, consisting of a small cask of gunpowder which was floated down the Hudson River into the British men-o-war, was also developed during the War of Independence. Buoys were made from casks for centuries, and in 1800 the Royal Navy used six standard types, the First Rate costing £1 13s. 1½d. and the Sixth Rate, 15s. 0½d.

Coopering thrived in Ireland, and coopers maintained their independence in this particular trade by establishing sizes of casks differing from their English counterparts by between one and six gallons. Their barrel was a 32-gallon vessel as compared with the English 36 and the kilderkin 16 to the English 18, and other casks varied similarly. Arthur Young, the first Minister of Agriculture for George III, in his book, *A Tour of Ireland with General Observations on the State of the Kingdom,* states that he saw seventy coopers at work in Cork. Not until 1701 did the coopers of Cork establish a guild, and shortly after this they were squabbling over objections to the employment of Catholic coopers. Cork was a very busy port. In 1771, 118,169 barrels of beef, 23,381 of pork and 92,802 firkins of butter were among its exports.

In Scotland during the eighteenth century vessels known as bickers were made with staves of alternate contrasting light and dark woods, and hooped with willow strands. The staves were feathered into each other, and it is said that the only tool used in making them was a penknife. Drinking-vessels for spirits, known as quaiches, were also made in this way, and can be seen in most of the Scottish folk museums, (fig. 79); salt boxes for the table were made similarly.

At *pl. 86* is a photograph of the Coopers' Hall, King Street, Bristol, which the Coopers Company of Bristol built around 1750, but later found themselves so impoverished that they let, and then sold in 1785, leaving to posterity a wonderful classic façade with Corinthian columns and pediments to be used as a fruit market and for auction sales and all manner of financially worthy functions though still retaining the name Coopers Hall.

The cooper in the days of Pyne was a very busy man; the industrial revolution had yet to get under way, and at *pl. 90* Pyne, in his inimitable way, portrays him at work.

79. Whisky quaich, Scottish, eighteenth century
(Approximately ⅔ actual size)

CHAPTER FOURTEEN

The Nineteenth Century

It was during this last century that the whole pattern of life in England, which had changed so little through the centuries, began to alter dramatically. The revolution brought about by steam power gathered momentum, and in consequence many old and honoured trades went down before the machine, and countrymen were forced to serve their conquerors in the choking towns. Cheap galvanized iron, and later cheap tinned or enamelled steel buckets, bowls and drums began to flood the markets, so that most of the white coopers succumbed to this unequal competition. The wet cooper's casks were still in demand, but here, machinery, at first crude, but later adequate, began to be employed. It was soon satisfactory in making rough, cheap, dry casks.

Although patents had been taken out much earlier, the first machines were not used in cooperages until the 1850s. They consisted of steam-powered saws and drills, which did the less skilled jobs, and were generally accepted as an aide to the cooper. But by the 1890s machinery had been developed and perfected to such an extent that the wet coopers saw it as a rival menacing their jobs, and some hostility developed.

The nineteenth century virtually saw the end of the village cooper. In the 1853 Commercial Directory for Bedfordshire fifteen were listed; in 1861 there were fourteen; by 1871 there were only nine and in 1894, three. The 1910 Directory had only one cooper in its pages. During this period the population of the county doubled. Many of these coopers were combining their trade with malting or brewing, or retailing beer; Thomas Foster of George Street, Luton, was also a seedsman, and Thomas Wingrove, a furniture broker. Village coopers commonly turned their hand to allied woodwork, as the following advertisement which appeared over the cooper's shop at Hailsham, Sussex, early in the century, will confirm:

As other people have a sign,
I say—just stop and look at mine!

Here, Wratten, cooper, lives and makes
Ox bows, trug-baskets, and hay-rakes.
Sells shovels, both for flour and corn,
And shauls, and makes a good box-churn,
Ladles, dishes, spoons and skimmers,
Trenchers too, for use at dinners.
I make and mend both tub and cask,
And hoop 'em strong, to make them last.
Here's butter prints, and butter scales,
And butter boards, and milking pails.
N'on this my friends may safely rest—
In serving them I'll do my best;
Then all that buy, I'll use them well
Because I make my goods to sell.

There was no 'built-in obsolescence' here. Had you walked into his shop you would most probably have seen hams and sides of bacon hanging up in the chimney corner; oak chippings and sawdust from the larger cooperages were by-products sold to the fish-curers. A few of these coopers became general coopers dealing in second-hand brewers' casks as did Bob Jones, of Brackley, Northants., who was still in business in the 1940s.

The dry coopers, too, were losing ground rapidly to the manufacturers of metal drums and tins, and they suffered a great blow with the introduction of refrigeration aboard ships whereby meat did not need to be salted in casks, at around 1870. This naturally affected the Coopers' Guild of Cork. During the nineteenth century they had laid down rules for apprentices, insisting upon five-year terms from the age of fourteen when the boy had to be capable of reading and writing. The hours worked were from six until six in the summer and during the hours of daylight in the winter. A census of 1830 showed that seventy-four coopers were living in Cork, but by 1944 the number had dropped to forty. In 1883 there were seven exhibits of coopers' work at the Annual Cork Fair, and it was reported that they did not give the impression of a vigorous growing trade.' A catalogue for the 1932 Fair listed only one coopering exhibitor. Credit must be given to the Irish coopers for their foresight in establishing a benevolent society in 1886 which numbered among its benefits emigration expenses to coopers.

From the time of the Napoleonic Wars Ireland had exported stout to England, and by 1868, 255,000 hogsheads (382,500 barrels) were exported to England yearly, at 57s. a hogshead. In addition to this there was the beer and stout consumed at home which, with regard to the small population, was enormous, insomuch that it was said that, 'The full casks going from Dublin, and the returned empty casks, played a role in the Irish rural railway economy similar to that of coal in England.'

Transporting costs were therefore high, and the Guinness brewery reckoned a cask to average four journeys in a year. Their casks had a life of ten years, and were costing £2 each to make, and maintain at this time. They were spending £26,000 a year on cooperage, making about 34,000 casks, breaking up 9,000 and keeping 100,000 in repair.

At the beginning of the century life in the Navy was very much the same as it had been in the preceding two or three centuries, and Jimmy Bungs, as the ship's cooper was nicknamed, was an important member of the crew of any ship. Article xii of *Admiralty Instructions* dated 1808 stated,

The very great demand for beer and water casks at the out ports are making it extremely difficult, more especially in time of war, to raise and fit them fast enough, and the expense attending the same being very great, and as both the difficulty and expense would be materially lessened if the beer and water casks were not to be shaken, never to suffer them to be shaken unless in absolute necessity, or taken to pieces.

Again, other orders condemn the use of 'improper violence' with casks; Article xxxix stated '. . . it is of the greatest moment that the strictest attention should be paid to the due preservation of casks, staves and hoops of every description'. Another Article of 1808 ordered that all beer and water casks for ships leaving on foreign service were to be new in order to prevent the buying of casks abroad. The Navy had been forced by numerous complaints, particularly the heavy expense of cooperage at Madras, and in the Presidencies of India, to raise the pay of coopers on board ships in order to attract better men. In the three coopering ranks a master cooper was to receive £2 5s. 6d., a cooper's mate £1 18s. 6d. and a cooper's crew £1 15s. 6d., which compared favourably with other tradesmen. The establishment of the first four ships of the line was four coopers in each, a fifth ship of the line three coopers, a sixth two and a sloop one.

But events were already surreptitiously working against the cooper. At this time sailors in the Navy received grog, one part rum to three parts water, twice a day; they had been enjoying this since 1692, plus one gallon of small (weak) beer. A letter from the Office for Revising the Civil Affairs of His Majesty's Navy, dated 7 September 1805, suggested that it would be,

'. . . very beneficial in the public service and tend greatly to preserve the health of ships crews if, in lieu of the gallon of small beer now allowed, two quarts of ale made from the same proportion of malt and hops (were substituted) enabling the ships with great convenience to put to sea . . . for five or six weeks. To be served twice a day as is grog. . . . saving space, labour, fuel, casks and cooperage.'

The Master Brewers and Master Coopers of Plymouth and Portsmouth were asked for their opinions: The brewers stated that costs would not be greatly reduced by this, from their point of view, and the coopers, perhaps recognizing the 'thin end of the wedge', were noncommittal. Today neither beer nor grog is issued to sailors. *Pl. 87,* 31 July 1970, shows the last issue of grog on board one of Her Majesty's ships. It was described by the Admiralty as an anachronism that had persisted into the twentieth century, and the coopers of the Naval Depot, who had perpetuated this anachronism, moved to the last remaining part of the trade, whisky barrels.

An Admiralty Article of 1861 gave instructions that 'On the first fitting out of every ship or vessel to be hereafter commissioned he (the Quartermaster) is to demand from Her Majesty's Stores a set of cooper's tools, large if for foreign, and small if for home service'. The set consisted of a bick iron, bolster (chince), bung borer, chalk, vice, driver, extra helves (wooden handles) flags, gimlet, marking irons, punch, rivets, and striking hammer'.

Coopers who supplied their own tools (duly certified) were paid an extra twopence a day.

The number of casks used on board ships in 1861 was considerable. There were harness casks, casks with their top heads hinged for all manner of storage, steep casks for cooks, match and top tubs, wash-deck and urine tubs, covered buckets and utensils for sick-bay, mess barricoes, fire buckets and bread bins and even spittoons (see *pl. 93,* of coopered naval utensils).

Article xix of 1861 stated that a cooper needed to be examined by the Master Cooper of the Victualling Yard to establish whether he was qualified to perform. This had been the case for many years, but in 1887 an Admiralty Article gave details of an examination to be passed whereby a cooper had to establish his fitness for the rating, to have had sufficient experience in the trade, to be of good character and to be able to read and write 'fairly'.

Water casks of butt, punch, hogshead and half-hogshead size were still in use in 1887, and an Article of that year stated that iron-bound casks were all to be accounted for, and when out of use to be sent home, indicating their continuing value. However metal tanks were gradually replacing casks for the storage of water, and refrigeration and different packaging methods were coming into being.

Civilian coopers employed by the Admiralty in the victualling yards enjoyed a security far above that of coopers working in the town trade, as other coopers' jobs were called, and watched their wages as carefully as any modern trade unionist.

The Deptford block coopers, piecework coopers, had petitioned the Admiralty for an increase in price for making dry casks out of English beech when cheap foreign timber became unobtainable because of the the war in 1794. This was granted, but taken away in April 1804, when the beech was worked up, so they again petitioned for equal pay with the town trade. When this was granted the price of cheese casks was omitted from the list, the Master Cooper deciding that he could get the apprentices to make them at the old rate. This caused another petition to be sent to the Admiralty in 1805, and granted. Thomas Kelsey, the Master Cooper in Dover, was sixty years old in 1805 when, because of age and infirmity, he asked to be superannuated. He had been in Admiralty service for forty-six years, thirteen at Portsmouth as a block cooper, where he had served his apprenticeship, one at Deptford and twenty-five as Master Cooper in Dover. He was given £60 per annum. In a similar position Mr Howitson of Deptford, First Foreman of the Cooperage, then nearly seventy and with fifty years' service, was granted £64 per annum. It was said that he had been earning an average of £185 16s. 0d. per annum. The pay of a labourer at this time was around 15s. a week.

In the West India Docks, Port of London, alone, hundreds of coopers were being employed at the turn of the century. There were rum coopers and sugar coopers, the rum work being 'wet' and therefore requiring more skill than the sugar, 'dry' work. 'Extra coopers' were also given employment by the day, or for a half or quarter of a day. Their pay had been 6s. a day during the war, but was reduced to 5s. a day in 1816, and they worked from eight in the morning until four in the afternoon, with a twenty minute break. Many of the rum coopers, working piecework, earned up to 10s. a day, four times as much as a labourer of those times.

On 4 August 1821, because of congestion at the gates when the workers left the docks, the dock management made a ruling that the sugar coopers must not leave the docks until four minutes past four o'clock, so as to ease the situation. This seemingly innocuous order proved to be the spark which ignited all the other grievances that had been rankling for years, and on the evening of the seventh the sugar coopers went out on strike. It was, of course, in violation of the Combination Acts of 1799. John Smith, a rum cooper, called a meeting in the 'Angel', in the Minories, and promised that the rum coopers and town coopers at work would each contribute 2s. 6d. a week towards the strike, and that the strikers would receive 3s. a day, with the backing of the Coopers' Friendly Society. To break the strike the Principal Master Cooper met the strikers in a field by the docks and said that those coopers who did not answer to their names and go back to work would not be admitted into the docks again. His demands met with no response from the disenchanted coopers.

On the eighth the rum coopers petitioned the directors of the West India Docks Company in the following words, summing up their grievances:

To the Honorable, the Directors of the West India Dock Company. The humble petition of the coopers on the rum-quay sheweth:

That your petitioners, on former occasions, received from your Honorable Board, the sum of six shillings per day for their labour, in the capacity of their trade.

That your Honorable Board have thought expedient to decrease the above humble petitioners of one shilling per day, and thereby greatly injure the wives and families of an honest and industrious class of tradesmen.

That your petitioners humbly conceive their earnings would amount (in the event of working by the piece) to nearly double the amount of their present wages.

That your petitioners most submissively request the favour of being reinstated at their former wages of six shillings per day in order that they may be enabled to support with credit themselves and families.

That your petitioners beg leave to state, that they either individually or collectively, are ready to prove at your Honorable Board, the before mentioned allegations, when it shall please your Honorable Board to command us, or any of us, so to do.

And your petitioners as in duty bound will ever pray, etc., etc.

The respectful prudence exhibited in this rather quaint petition contrasts with the attitude of today's massive unions; they have come a long way.

Very soon there were ninety-five ships of sugar held up in the docks.

The rum coopers were promised 7s. 6d. a day if they would work on the sugar side, a very tempting offer, but they refused to a man. The directors of the docks, becoming rather desperate, then sent to Bristol and Liverpool offering to pay the expenses of coopers willing to work in London. At this time coopers working in the Bristol Docks were being paid 3s. 6d. a day, working from six until six. To these people the offer must have seemed very attractive. However, the London coopers were aware of this move on the part of the management, and one of their leaders, Walter Foreman, also travelled to Bristol, where he addressed the dock coopers at a meeting in the 'Hole in the Wall' Public House, now the 'Merchant's Arms'.

Only twenty-eight coopers actually arrived in London from Bristol, and these were 'entertained' by the striking coopers, and did not turn up at the docks, so the management failed to break the strike in this way. However, the end was in sight because, despite the promises of the strike organizers, the strikers received only 7s. at the end of the first week, and 4s. at the end of the second, and they found themselves being starved into submission. The justifiable militancy of these early unions could never be supported adequately, as their finances were not given time to accumulate. On 23 August the men returned to work, defeated, the management refusing to negotiate or to give any pledges whatsoever.

The sequel was played out on 13 December 1821, when four coopers, John Smith, Walter Foreman, Samuel Hucks and Daniel Hall were arraigned before the Common Serjeant on trial, indicted on sixteen counts for conspiracy, 'in that, together with divers other evil disposed persons . . . of the art, trade and manual occupation of a cooper . . . to extort great sums of money for their labour . . . did desist and totally leave their labour . . .' The coopers' case was that the management had conspired in 1816 to reduce their pay, and later to alter the hours and conditions, and that they would have been guilty only if they had refused to contribute towards the strikers who would otherwise have starved. Their defence was spirited and noble and won the sympathy of the majority of the public. The jury, after careful deliberation, returned a verdict of 'Not Guilty'. A drawing of sugar casks being unloaded is at *pl. 92*.

The coopers were among the pioneers of the trade-union movement, who ignored the law when they considered it to be unjust. In 1813 the London coopers agreed with employers' representatives in the establishing of a List Price which fixed piecework prices, and these were kept for many years with periodical percentage increases due to the cost of living.

After the Napoleonic Wars the question of the slave trade, which had brought great prosperity to Bristol until it was banned in 1807, and increased shipping dues, imposed by a government intent upon ending direct taxation, caused a great depression in trade in this area, and the coopers, who were affected considerably, banded together in 1822 to form a society which they called the 'Friends of Humanity'. The Preamble to the Rules of the Society reads:

To members of a trade who by their daily intercourse with one another are made acquainted with each other's circumstances, it is unnecessary to urge any reason in support of the objects set forth, and which are hereinafter specified. All must be impressed with the conviction that it is both a moral and Christian obligation to relieve the distress of our fellow-operatives, while by so doing each individual member is also providing for himself a guarantee against the vicissitudes and calamities to which all more or less are liable. To achieve these laudable objects, the trade from which we draw our resources to enable us to sustain them must be in a healthy state, and we are determined to wield no weapon of violence or injustice in our defence, but to use our moral energies combined for the accomplishment of this our honest aim; and the better to preserve order and regularity in our proceedings we agree to be regulated by the following rules (*pl. 91*).

On the lines of a mutual aid society its objects were to give relief to members who sustained loss by fire, to support the aged, and to pay for the burial of its dead. There were, at first, no sick or out-of-work benefits. Contributions were 1s. a month, and 2s. 6d. a week was paid to superannuated members, while members received death benefits of £8, £5 for a wife. A Superintendent presided over the society, helped by a clerk who performed the office of secretary. The landlord of the meeting-house was treasurer. The members agreed to subscribe and not to draw on the funds as far as possible in order to establish the society on a strong financial footing. In 1832 the membership stood at 146, by 1868 300 members were on the books, by 1922 this was down to 250 again, and in 1945 it had dropped to a figure below 100. The Foreign Sugar Bounty and cheap beet sugar caused a depression in 1877, and many of the sugar cooperages did not survive; it was at this time that a resolution was passed, 'That in the opinion of this Conference the time had arrived when means should be adopted, whereby disputes between Employers and Employed would be settled without resorting to strikes.' Again the coopers were proving themselves pace-makers.

The first Bristol Price List was drawn out in 1856, and other small branches about the country drew up lists, varying slightly, after the London pattern.

Attempts were made to affiliate with other coopers' societies, and in 1861 a National Association of Coopers was formed, but this collapsed in 1870 through lack of funds. In 1878 the Mutual Association of Journeymen Coopers was floated, 'a loose collection of 32 societies with just a centre of communication', according to Sidney Webb. In October 1919 an Amalgamated Society of Coopers was formed with its head-quarters at Burton, and a Coopers Federation of Great Britain and Ireland based on London, having more bargaining power while allow-ing considerable local autonomy.

A charity originating in 1785 when Mrs Mary Packer gave £100 to the Company of Coopers of Bristol, the interest from which was to re-lieve the distress of poor widows of the Company, is still functioning.

Returning to London and the attitudes of the people of 1821, at the trial of the four dock coopers there was talk of working men being searched upon leaving the docks, and this, apparently, was not the case with 'respectable' men. Of the £200 which was received to pay for the strike 2½ guineas was collected at Barclay's Brewery, London.

It was around the turn of the century that some of the large brewery concerns which we know today began to emerge. The *Union Magazine and Imperial Register* for 1802 runs, 'Mr. Whitbread's brewery in Chis-well St. near Moorfields is the greatest in London . . . producing about 200,000 barrels of porter per year.' The popularity of porter, a strong, dark and heavily hopped beer, needing twelve months of maturation, caused the brewers to build large vats for this purpose, and even to compete with each other as did the early German princes.

An article in the *London Chronicle* of May 1787 told of a visit to the brewery by George III and Queen Charlotte, of large oak vats holding 3,500 barrels—'The great vessel at Heidelberg is nothing to these'—and of how the cooperage was looked at from an adjacent room; no doubt for some very good reason. This one brewery alone used 20,000 casks at the turn of the century.

The largest cooper-made vat on record was one holding 7,500 barrels 272,520 gallons, 30 ft. deep and 44 ft. in diameter, and this was raised in 1806 at the Meux Brewery in Clerkenwell. In the year 1814 a great porter vat, which had been the talk of London at the time of its

ANNO QUINQUAGESIMO QUINTO

GEORGII III. REGIS.

●●

C A P. CLXXXIX.

An Act for allowing *Henry Meux, Thomas Starling Benson, Florance Thomas Young, Richard Latham,* and *John Newberry,* to brew, Duty free, a Quantity of Strong Beer, the Duty on which will be equivalent to the Duty on the Beer loft, and to the Duties on the Malt and Hops expended in the Production of the Beer fo loft. [11th *July* 1815.]

WHEREAS on or about the Seventeenth Day of *October* One thoufand eight hundred and fourteen, Seven thoufand three hundred and fifty-five Barrels of Strong Beer, brewed within the laft preceding Year by *Henry Meux, Thomas Starling Benson, Florance Thomas Young, Richard Latham,* and *John Newberry,* Common Brewers, at their Brewhoufe in the Parifh of *Saint Giles in the Fields,* in the County of *Middlesex,* and for which Beer the Duties of Excife, amounting to Three thoufand three hundred and feventy-one Pounds had been duly paid, was, as is alledged by the faid *Henry Meux, Thomas Starling Benson, Florance Thomas Young, Richard Latham,* and *John Newberry,* loft by the accidental burfting of a Vat containing Part thereof, and the Staves of which burft Vat fell upon and broke off the Difcharge Cock of another Vat, and alfo broke a Pipe communicating with another Vat, fuch Two laft-mentioned Vats containing the Refidue of the faid Beer, and by the breaking of which Cock and Pipe the faid Refidue ran out and was loft, as is alfo alledged by the faid *Henry Meux, Thomas Starling Benson,*

19 G.   7   *Florance*

80. The first page of an Act of Parliament compensating for the duty paid on beer lost in the Vat Disaster.

81. A nineteenth-century vat house.

construction, burst its hoops. In the resulting flood and wild drunken orgy, with people 'flinging themselves on hands and knees to drink their fill', eight people were drowned or suffocated by the fumes of the old porter. Small tenements were flooded to such an extent that the walls collapsed as the liquor flowed along the streets. This vat was 22 ft. in height and contained 3,555 barrels. An Act of Parliament (fig. 80) needed to be passed to compensate Meux Brewery for the loss in duty paid. Following this disaster brewers began to cut the maturation period so as to use smaller vats, and later these were copper-lined, and very recently were made of stainless steel. A drawing of the Whitbread Vat House of 1873 is at fig. 81.

The amount of beer brewed in this country at the end of the seventeenth century was around 20 million gallons. This fell to 16 million during the depression following the Napoleonic Wars, but reached 30 in the 'golden age', rising to 37 million gallons at the end of the nineteenth century. We now consume around 30, but, of course, the population has risen considerably.

Exports, which before the French Wars were running at around 125,000 barrels yearly, dropped to 100,000, which was partly due to discriminate taxation in Ireland which virtually stopped all English beer imports, but by the middle of the century we were exporting 400,000 barrels a year, much of this to India. Coopers engaged on wet work for brewers were therefore thriving.

Bass's Brewery at Burton on Trent employed 400 coopers in 1889. Their staves, weathering before being made into casks, occupied 25 acres of ground. Annually they would use 700 tons of hoop iron. In an inventory of 1889 there were 40,499 butts, 133,464 hogsheads, 127,592 barrels, 147,969 kilderkins and 68,587 firkins, 518,121 casks in all; 25,000 casks were exported yearly, which, end to end, would have stretched for fifteen miles, and those delivered to depots in the United Kingdom would similarly have stretched from London to Edinburgh. They had a steam cooperage with machinery for most of the processes involved in cask manufacture, and could produce 2,000 casks a week (*pl. 30*). During slack periods thousands of new casks were made and stacked aside for months before being put into use, when they had to be driven tight where the wood had shrunk. At this time firms were not run by accountants with their fine marginal costing, and shareholders considered 5 per cent a good return on their investment. Breweries regarded themselves as family concerns, as indeed the majority were, and they were prepared to accept financial loss rather than lay people off work, when they would literally starve. The market was growing fast with the expanding population, most houses were tied to the breweries, and therefore competition was negligible in most cases. Samuel Allsop and Sons of Burton employed 120 coopers with 5 acres of land devoted to cooperage, and a steam mill.

The larger London breweries employed upwards of a hundred

coopers. In addition to these there were a vast number of small breweries, many so small that they needed to employ a cooper for only a few months of the year, generally just before the busy season, and so gave work to a number of travelling coopers. Many, like the cooper of Turvey, Bedfordshire (fig. 82), would have been 'jacks of all trades', and perhaps not many of them would have been capable of commending themselves to their employers as did William Dalley. Most of these small breweries employed coppers loaned from cooperages, more expensive perhaps, but far more reliable.

William Dalley of Turvey, plough-wright, Cooper, and Carpenter; drawn from life April 1830. He having worked for the writer thirty five years.

Ob. April 16ᵗʰ 1837.

82. A nineteenth-century travelling cooper.

At *pl. 44* is a travelling cooper's jointer, made so that it can be carried in two parts.

Certain large cooperages also began to emerge in the nineteenth century. Shooters, Chippingdale and Colliers of London were employing 630 coopers at the end of the century. Wilson's Cooperage at Bermondsey concentrated, during the early part of the century, on water and sperm oil casks, but as the demand dropped turned to the growing brewing industry for its outlet. The David Roberts Cooperage at

Tottenham was employing over sixty coopers in the 1860s, making casks and vats for brewers, vinegar brewers, laundries and sugar-refiners. They had seven two-horse vans and four one-horse vans, a wagonette and four horses.

In the 1890s there was growing discontent among the London coopers, brought about for a number of reasons. The railways, with their cheap freight rates, were bringing casks into London from the provincial centres, notably Burton and Bristol, and from Scotland, where cheaper wage rates in these areas made their casks very competitive. The London coopers also had their jobs threatened by the increasing use of machines. Machine-made casks were finding their way into this country from Germany; but worse was foreseen when one London brewery started to install a machine shop capable of manufacturing casks from start to finish without needing the skill of a cooper. In the autumn of 1890 the journeymen coopers of London negotiated a 10 per cent increase in pay upon the list prices of 1886, which had superseded the 1813 Price List. This piecework price concerned most of the coopering in London; only on small breweries, on ships, or in the case of temporary work was 'day work' done at a fixed rate of pay according to the amount of time worked. Of course it must be realized that a cooper's earnings at piecework depended, to a large extent, upon the quality of the wood with which he had to work. The Crown Memel oak was excellent wood, but occasionally one would find 'brack' and sawn staves amongst it which should have been thrown out, and this is difficult to work with and tends to crack upon being bent, giving the cooper a tremendous amount of extra work for which he did not receive any pay. Complaints about the quality of the timber were becoming more numerous, and so in June 1891 the coopers presented the masters with a new list defining the various types of timber in order to compensate for this 'brack' with a better price. To this the masters, after much time-wasting deliberation, could not agree, and there was deadlock. On 14 September the journeymen coopers of London went out on strike. Long letters were exchanged, and the atmosphere was at all times most cordial, if lethargic, for September starts the slack period for coopers, following the thirsty and demanding summer, and so from this point of view the strike was badly timed. Strike pay from the Union was small and there were no state welfare benefits to fall back upon, so that, while some may have managed on their savings, others suffered great privation or worked out of their trade at any work available. For almost three months the coopers and masters stood their ground; neither side would give until, with Christmas approaching and stomachs empty, the coopers agreed to return to work on 7 December, having achieved nothing. One of these strikers, Jack Fenner, obtained work on a merchantman during the strike and was subsequently black-listed by the Union, which was very strong in London. He then went to Banbury, where he worked for Kilby's Cooperage, which at that time was employing about thirty coopers.

It can be seen from the nineteenth-century apprenticeship indenture (fig. 84) that the length of an apprenticeship had been cut to four years, and with Victorian practicality, if an apprentice could make a cask in a workmanlike manner within that time he would be paid his 'thirds', which was one-third of what he earned, for half of the remainder of his apprenticeship, and then two-thirds of what he earned. Mr Roberts, the founder of the cooperage in Tottenham, only served eighteen months in his apprenticeship in London in 1850, being paid half of his earnings for one year, and then two-thirds for the last six months.

Although the payment of 'thirds' was very common throughout the trade, Rubin Burman served his apprenticeship at Trueman's Brewery in London from 1848 to 1855, on the promise that he would be clothed and fed, and until he was twenty-one he never had so much as a shilling in his pocket. He moved to Salt's Brewery, Burton, and worked there until 1889, when, at the age of 55, he started on his own in Hawkins Lane, Burton. His cooperage, now operating under the name of John Grout and Sons, a large cooperage which was bought in 1938, is the only one still in existence in Burton, the home of brewing.

83. Stephenson's Rocket.

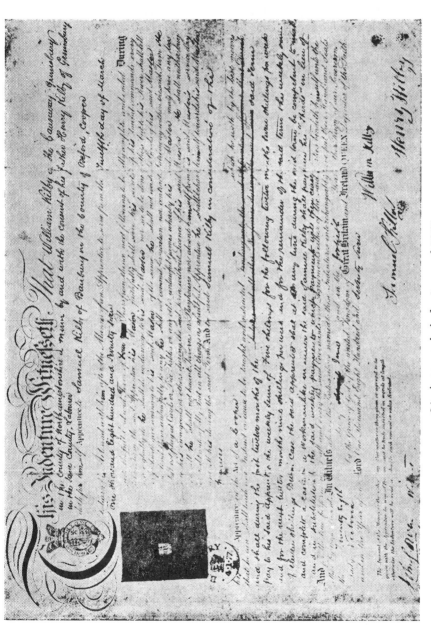

84. A cooper's indentures of 1877.

A French cooper from Cadillac settled in Los Angeles, U.S.A., in 1829. His name was Jean Louis Vigne and he planted a 100-acre vineyard with about 100,000 vines brought specially from France. Until this time the Spanish Fathers had used roughly made Indian earthenware vessels for their wine and had transported it in leather bottles after the very ancient manner. Vigne was able to build maturing vats and casks with the local oak, and in the European style send his heavy wines in casks as ballast round the Horn to Boston, maturing as they went, and so built up a splendid business. In the words of Edward Hyams, '. . . this introduction of coopering brought about a revolution in Californian wine-handling which repeated that which had occurred in France and Italy some sixteen centuries earlier'.

It was natural for the first trains to carry their water in large casks (fig. 83).

The 'Empire Style' wine cooler (fig. 85), together with aspidistra pots, was quite popular in the nineteenth century.

When an Admiral or person of high rank died at sea, in order to get his body home it was often necessary to put it in a cask of brandy, so that the body was, in effect, pickled. On one such ship, sailing home, some of the seamen were found to be the worse for drink, and upon questioning them they admitted that they had been 'tapping the Admiral'.

85. An Empire style wine cooler.

91. The Arms of the Friends of Humanity, Bristol Coopers' Society

92. The sugar trade

93. Coopered vessels used by each mess in a
nineteenth-century 'man o' war'

94. The Coopers of Banbury, 1913

95. The last cooper to pass out in the Company
of London

96. The great herring trade, Yarmouth docks, 1954

97. Scottish girls packing herrings, Yarmouth 1954

98. A bever barrel

99. The cooperage

100, 101. Across arid lands and in northern forests coopered vessels
were used extensively up until the turn of the
century

102. The beginning

103. And the end

104. Late nineteenth-century hand operated
washing machine

105. The end of an age-old trade

CHAPTER FIFTEEN

And the Ending

While many other old tradesmen were laying down their tools, and quietly submitting to the superiority of twentieth-century technology, the wet cooper, in all his antiquity, was still there at the block, practising an art and craft that was defying this industrial revolution.

He would usually start at six in the morning, break off for breakfast, bever and dinner, and finish at six in the evening, and during that time he would have made as many as four firkins or two barrels out of stout timber. He would have sweated and slogged and used his skill to the utmost, and earned his money which at this time would have amounted to about three pounds a week, three times as much as a labourer. Day work was never so highly paid, and if a cooper on piece work was 'called from the block' to do unpriced work on casks, he would have insisted on a rate higher than that of the day work hourly pay. The picture at *pl. 94* shows the coopers of Sam. Kilby and Sons, Banbury, and is dated 1913.

A cooper having an apprentice would receive their joint earnings and give his apprentice a few shillings at the end of the week, and when the apprentice started on his 'thirds' the employer had a share of the remainder as payment for his patronage. Few apprentices were exploited. When a cooper came 'out of his time', that is, finished his apprenticeship, it was customary for him to go through a form of initiation, a ceremony which must have been performed as a matter of celebration by the first apprentices of the Guild, after they had passed the examination of the wardens, if not by earlier ones. The apprentice would raise-up a barrel and call, 'Truss Oh!', but instead of his mates helping him to fire the cask they would pitch him into it in place of the cresset. They would then proceed to fire the cask, driving the truss hoops until it began to take shape, and all the while shouting their congratulations and other rather humorous comments. The more exuberant would then throw shavings and anything else within reach, over the initiate, crouched there, deafened and covered with all the mess that he had made, but perhaps inwardly thankful knowing that he had reached the end of a hard road. He would then be rolled along in his barrel the length of the shop, and be tipped out, a fully fledged journeyman cooper. 'Drinks all round', he would gasp thankfully. In the fifties and sixties, with the end of brewery coopering in sight, the brewers made much of the passing-out of their coopers, and pictures like the one at *pl. 95* appeared every year or so, showing incidentally the last cooper officially indentured under the rules of the Coopers' Livery Company, Steve Holterman of Haig's Cooperage, being tossed out of his cask, in this case an old sherry butt which had been substituted.

86. The Chinese dipper.

The Annual Works Outing was eventually replaced in the thirties by the one-week holiday, and then after the 1939 War the two weeks' holiday, and the absenteeism which followed the week-end of deep drinking, called 'playing a day', seemed to go out of fashion between the wars with the depression. Breweries did not suffer as much as other industries during the depression, though whisky coopering virtually came to a halt, and in Scotland there was some ill-feeling between the coopers, where the Glasgow whisky coopers accused the Edinburgh brewing coopers of a lack of understanding. Brewery coopers in Scotland worked a system of task work during this period, whereby each cooper repaired two casks per day irrespective of the extent of the job and was paid at a fixed rate for each cask. A summary of the trade as reported by branches of the Coopers Amalgamated Union for August 1938 is printed below:

	Number of members	State of trade	Number unem- ployed	On short time
Aberdeen	36	Bad	9	—
Alloa	66	Fair	8	—
Belfast	60	Bad	16	4
B'ham & W'hampton	122	Fair	3	7
Bradford	86	Bad	7	8
Bristol	90	Bad	9	10
Dundee	24	Bad	6	2
Gateshead	23	Bad	9	—
Glasgow	500	Bad	27	30
Greenock	36	Bad	4	8
Hull	138	Fair	8	4
Leeds	58	Fair	2	—
Liverpool D. & T.	45	Bad	17	7
Livingston	15	Bad	2	8
Newcastle upon Tyne	60	Bad	5	4
Nottingham	13	Good	—	—
Potteries	12	Bad	1	1
Runcorn	10	Bad	—	10
Sheffield	33	Fair	2	1
St Helens	17	Bad	2	9
Swansea	29	Bad	3	1
Warrington	42	Bad	4	16
Widnes	85	Bad	14	21

Similar economic forces were affecting the coopers of America, where an enormous number of casks were used for corn- and meat-packing, resins, turpentine and pitch as well as beer, wines and spirits. A tremendous fillip came the way of American coopers with the rise of the petroleum industry, where the demand for casks was so great that old whisky casks were used, and oil magnates were buying forests to ensure a supply of timber for their coopers, producing 42-gallon casks. Hildegard Dolson wrote of how early oil towns could be described as '. . . one main street, filthy and snarling, with piles of barrels in lurching pyramids wherever you look . . . and the river was teeming with flatboats and barges, all greasy, all with barrels banging about'. Oil ran away to waste when coopers were unable to keep up with the pace of the gushers. Large wooden vats covered acres of ground in the early refineries. The care taken with oil samples sent abroad can be measured by this extract from an exporter to his manager, '. . . to select the very best barrels (your new ones) paint and dry the heads thoroughly and nicely, put on the Plate with the Trade Mark in the most skillful manner, hoops, etc., thoroughly secured, and well fitted for a voyage to

Europe . . .'. The demand ended more quickly than it had begun, casks being replaced by 55-gallon, mass-produced, steel drums. At a time when wet coopering at least was still viable prohibition dealt a terrible blow to the trade.

In China and the Orient barrels were only used where they had been imported containing a foreign product. Drinks are not exported, and earthenware jars and carboys in large wicker baskets were common, but a type of bucket with one stave proud for a handle, and one shaped for a spout, and called a dipper, was used quite extensively. Bamboo was woven to make hoops. The Chinese cooper used similar tools to our jointer, downright and stoup plane, together with a two-handled croze. They have now started making softwood eighteen-gallon casks by machinery for shipping ginger through Hong Kong. The dipper is shown at fig. 86.

In other parts of the world, Russia and Canada in particular, buckets were often made with the widest part at the bottom (fig. 87).

87. A Russian peasant with yoke and buckets.

The Royal Navy still needed coopers aboard their ships, until after the Great War because, although casks were not now used for water or beer, there were still the rum puncheons, bread-bins, wooden buckets in the magazines and breakers or barricoes for the lifeboats. The holds of some of the famous 'Q' ships were filled with empty casks intended to make the ships unsinkable. With one that did sink casks were released from a great depth and shot to the surface, causing havoc among rescuers.

Before the 1939–45 War when Memel oak was still being imported into the Surrey Docks, coopers collecting their timber would always take a small cask of beer for the dockers, in order to ensure preferential treatment.

In 1898 a practice called 'grogging' was officially prohibited by Customs, though certainly not stopped. When a cooper came across a freshly emptied cask of brandy, or similar spirit, he would pour a gallon or so of boiling water into it, shake it up and then let it stand for an hour or more. He would then find himself in possession of a gallon of quite strong spirit, similar perhaps to the Navy's grog, part spirit, part water, whence the name 'grogging'. As well as cheating the customs it was thought to be detrimental to the cask.

A considerable trade has been carried on for centuries in salted fish. As early as 1280 Aberdeen exported salmon and other fish, and we have read how in the Middle Ages regulations were passed governing the size and quality of fish casks, but it was the Dutch who really exploited the herring, for as soon as the shoals moved from the Baltic to the North Sea in the fourteenth century they had factory ships with coopers on board operating there. It became known as the Dutch Gold Mine. They started factories in Scotland in the early nineteenth century, and the industry was brought south to East Anglia by the Scottish Curers. Hundreds of coopers were employed in the making of herring barrels—slight, soft-wood casks, referred to as dry-tight work. By 1913 the trade had reached its peak and there were fifteen factories turning out over a million barrels a year, and in addition some 1,500 coopers were making casks by hand for six months of the year, and during the season they would supervise and head-up the casks, moving south with the fishing fleets. Then came the Great War, the Russian revolution and the devaluation of the German mark; the market collapsed. Between the wars the trade, though not inconsiderable, was much less, dropping from 1.4 million cran in 1913 to 1 million in 1924 and to 750,000 in 1937. Its value dropped even more, from £2 million to just over £800,000, between 1924 and 1937, and the barrels cured from 845,475 in 1924 to 495,000 in 1937. The second world war disrupted the industry again, and after the war, in the 1950s, the herring shoals moved away, some thought because of overfishing by the Russian fleets which had begun to invade the North Sea fisheries, so that in 1953 only 114,000 barrels were exported, and in 1954 67,000, while today, with the exception of an occasional shipload to Australia the herring industry of East Anglia is finished as far as coopering is concerned. Where 1,600 steam drifters, plus many smaller craft, operated from Yarmouth and Lowestoft in 1913, during the autumn of 1968 there were only two. Between 40,000 and 50,000 barrels are still being made in Scotland covering the needs of the Scottish exporters, but few apprentices have entered the trade since the war; the average age of the fifty or so coopers still working is around sixty.

These coopers had a four-year apprenticeship, their pay rising from 35 per cent to 75 per cent of a journeyman's wage during that time. They worked day work and by the piece and belonged to a coopers' section of the Transport and General Workers Union, who made a ruling that every employer had to use 500 hand-made casks for every cooper he employed before putting machine-made casks into use. Herring-barrel coopers were never recognized by the Coopers Union. Russia was by far the largest customer for our herring, and consequently the work was nicknamed Klondyking. It was possible for a cooper, like Mr Robertson of Yarmouth, to witness the industry declining from its peak in 1913, when he started work at 4s. a week as a cooper apprentice, to its demise when he retired in 1965; a very frustrating experience for any man (*pls. 96* and *97*).

A common item of equipment for farmers, and people working on the land in this country, was the bever barrel, sometimes called a costrel, and holding anything from 2 pints to a gallon of beer (*pl. 98*). It could be slung over the shoulder to carry into the fields, and it had a protruding mouthpiece, part of the bung stave left proud, with a vent hole in the next stave. These date from the Middle Ages. The increase in beer duties during the Great War and the poverty among farm workers following it caused this custom to come to an end, but brewers continued to supply farmers with diluted beer at harvest-time in large casks. The word 'bever' comes from the Old French word *beivre*, meaning drinking, and is still used by countrymen in Hertfordshire for 'elevenses'. At Harvard, America, students in the mid-seventeenth century would have two meals a day, plus two bevers of bread and beer. The morning break of workers in a cooperage or brewery was called a bever, and an issue of beer was made from the 'chapel'. A typical small hand cooperage of the fifties is at (*pl. 99*).

The hand-operated washing machine of 1900 marked the end of another aspect of coopering (*pl. 104*).

A National Joint Industrial Council of the Cooperage Industry was formed in 1919, where representatives of coopers from branches in

London and District, Midlands, N.E. England and Yorkshire, S.W. England and S. Wales, N.W. England and N. Wales, West of Scotland and E. and N. Scotland met representatives of employers in the presence of a liaison officer from the Ministry of Labour. The decline in coopering gave the coopers little bargaining power, but, represented by very able men, agreement was reached amicably with regard to pay and conditions. Brewery coopering was coming to an end for many reasons.

From the time of the Great War increased duties caused brewers to concentrate on weaker beers for which less duty was payable, the alcoholic strength of the brew being the determining factor. Great care has to be taken with weak beers as they can very easily be contaminated by bacteria and wild yeast, and many small breweries with out-of-date plant, which could not easily be sterilized, were forced to sell out or merge. With the local restrictions on the granting of public-house licences the only way in which a brewery could expand, except in the free trade of clubs, was to buy another brewery, which it could use as a depot or close completely and sell for redevelopment, a most profitable exercise, and take over its pubs. Consequently a process of combination of increasing momentum came to the brewing industry, affecting the livelihood of the coopers. After the war of 1939–45 the popular beer was so weak that, far from deriving any benefit from maturing in oaken casks, it was more likely to become contaminated by wild yeast bacteria, able to live in the pores of the wood. Therefore the cleaning of casks became more and more important as the years progressed. Even before the 1939–45 war brewers had been searching for a container which could be sterilized and remain non-toxic. Lined metal casks seemed to be the answer, but brewers were worried about public reaction to their introduction, as this would be a departure from the traditional oaken casks whose very nature they had always advertised as giving flavour and quality to the beer. Consequently metal-lined wooden casks were the first to be introduced just after the war, but they were very expensive and not widely used. Laminated casks from Germany did not fit the bill.

Memel oak, used by almost all brewers' coopers until the 1939–45 War, became unobtainable, English oak was not regarded as completely satisfactory and that too was in short supply, Persian and American oaks did not fill the gap completely, and so in this respect problems were developing.

This vacuum, caused by timber shortage and price, was seized upon by certain small engineering firms which had mushroomed during the war making aluminium components for aircraft, and were now seeking outlets in peacetime requirements. Aluminium needed to be lined so as not to come into contact with the beer, and as soon as a suitable lining was found to withstand steam sterilization these drums began to be used, certain large brewers, notably Flowers of Luton, pioneering the way. They had the advantage of uniformity and were lighter than wooden ones. They were admirably fitted for pressure beer, where air is not allowed to come into contact with the beer before it is served, and therefore risk of infection is minimized.

The popularity of the bottle since the removal of the tax on glass in 1851 was now such that one-third of all beer sold in the 1950s was from the bottle. The coopers had had a champion in 1691 in Thomas Tryon, who said, ' . . . the bottle tinges or gives it (beer) a cold hard quality which is the nature of glass and stone . . . the cold Saturnine nature of the bottle has the greater power to tincture the liquor with its quality', but unfortunately in the long term his words had no effect. The can, in the form of 'pipkins' holding from four to seven pints, has replaced the once popular Christmas cask. The storage of these small pins for eleven months of the year was uneconomical by modern standards.

In the larger public houses tanks were fitted in the late fifties and early sixties so that beer could be supplied in bulk from tankers, again making the barrel obsolete.

It is estimated that the number of wooden casks used for ale and beer in this country was about 14½ million during the sixteenth century, rising to 18 million in the seventeenth, but with the increasing popularity of tea and other beverages this number dropped to 2,791,691 by 1940, and now, by reason of the foregoing, was virtually finished.

One after another during the 1950s and 1960s the independent cooperages and brewery cooperages began to close down. Certain wines for which there is a considerable demand are now being imported in fibre-glass tanks, and although coopered vessels are still required for the maturing of spirits, it is debatable how long it will be before modern science and technology find a less costly alternative process of maturation to make redundant the few remaining coopers.

With their fast-declining membership, from 900 London coopers in 1946, to 250 in 1969, and with around 2,500 over the whole country, the Coopers Union effected a nation-wide amalgamation of the independent societies in 1970. Each society has a different price list for pieceworkers and separate benevolent funds which they will retain until their usefulness is at an end. Mr James Whitton, secretary of the E. and N. Scotland Joint Industrial Council of the Cooperage Industry states, ' . . . brewery coopering and white coopering virtually does not exist in Scotland . . .' The Secretary of the South Wales coopers, Mr Lloyd, writes, '. . . We are down to seven members . . . engaged in knocking down casks . . . most coopers can adapt to anything, physical effort is nothing to a cooper . . .'

So, like so many grand old tradesmen, the wheelwrights, the chair-bodgers, the wood-turners and the blacksmiths, who laid down their tools between the wars, it is now the coopers who are going, and perhaps, in a generation or two a small boy will be asking, 'What's a barrel, Dad?'

Bibliography and Sources of Information

CHAPTER SIX

What Happened in History, Gordon Childe, 1942.
Ancient Europe, Stuart Piggot, p. 82, 1965.
Prehistoric England, Graham Clark, 1940.
Ancient Bronze Implements of Great Britain, J. Evans, 1881.
Discovering Archaeology in England and Wales, James Dyer, 1969.
The Tomb of Hesy, J. E. Quibell, p. 54, 1913.
Beni Hasan, P. E. Newberry, p. 12, 1893.
Dionysus, Edward Hyams, p. 167, 1965.
The Glastonbury Lake Village (vol. 1) Arthur Bulleid and H. St. George Gray, 1911.
Ashmolean Museum, Oxford. 260.
Manchester Museum. 1452, 1460–1–4–6, 1470.
British Museum. 1A, 6.86.

CHAPTER SEVEN

The Coopers' Company and Craft, Elkington, 1933.
The Later Roman Empire, A. H. M. Jones, 1964
The Cooperage Handbook, Hankerson, 1950.
The Ancient World, Luigi Pareti.
Decline and Fall of the Roman Empire, Gibbon.
A History of Technology (vol. 2), Oxford, 1957.
Notes on a Roman Cask, James Whitton, 1938.
Jewry Wall Museum, Leicester. *Dionysus*, Edward Hyams, 1965.
Reading City Museum.

CHAPTER EIGHT

The Beginnings of English Society, Dorothy Whitelock, 1952.
A History of English Ale and Beer, H. A. Monkton, 1966.
Ulster Journal of Archaeology, G. Bersu, 1947.
Archaeology Under Water, George F. Bass, 1966.
A History of the English Church and People, Bede, E. V. Rieu, 1955.

The Vikings, Johannes Brondsted, 1960.
Arthur and his Times, J. Lindsay, 1958.
The Devizes Museum.
The British Museum. AS 113–55, AS 17–45.
The Ashmolean Museum. 17 Leeds Room.

CHAPTER NINE

English Society in the Early Middle Ages, Stenton, 1951
Domesday Book to Magna Carta, Poole, 1951.
Feudal England, J. C. Holt.
Life in Norman England, Tomkeieff, 1966.
English Social History, Trevelyan, 1942.
Daily Living in the Twelfth Century, Madison, 1952.
A History of English Ale and Beer, Monkton, p. 39, 1966.
A History of Technology (vol. II), Oxford, 1957.
The Coopers' Company, Firth, 1848.
The Coopers' Company and Craft, Elkington, 1933.
Dionysus, E. Hyams, 1965.
Medieval London, Gwen A. Williams, 1963.
Fluctuations in the Anglo-Gascon Wine Trade, M. K. James.
London Letter Books B.
The English Townsman, Thomas Burke, 1946.

CHAPTER TEN

The Coopers' Company, J. F. Firth, 1848.
The Coopers' Company and Craft, G. Elkington, 1933.
'Paris Bibliothèque Nationale MS', lat. 11015, f. 10.
The Armorial Bearings of the Several Incorporated Companies of Newcastle on Tyne, James Walker and M. A. Richardson, 1824.
Acts and Charters of the Incorporate Trade of Coopers of Glasgow, Aird and Coghill, 1885.
The Cooper Craft, William Craig, 1899.
The Incorporated Trades of Edinburgh, James Colston, 1891.
Perth's Old Time Trades and Trading, Peter Barter, 1930.
Victoria, County History of Yorkshire, The City of York, Ed. R. B. Pugh, 1961.

CHAPTER ELEVEN

The Coopers' Company, J. F. Firth, 1848.
A Short History of the Worshipful Company of Coopers of London, Sir William Foster, 1944.
The Coopers' Company and Craft, G. Elkington, 1933.

The British Museum MS, Harley, 1996.

A History of English Ale and Beer, H. A. Monkton, p. 98, 1966.

The British Museum MS. Lansdown 46, 110.

Drake, Ernle Bradford, p. 111, 1965.

Description of Britaine, Harrison, 1577.

Coventry Leet Book 1420–1555 (trans. Mary Dormer Harris) fol. 306. 782/132.

The Armorial Bearings of the Companies of Newcastle, Walker and Richardson, 1824.

The Incorporated Trades of Edinburgh, James Colston, 1891.

Acts and Charters of the Incorporation of Coopers of Glasgow, Pub. Aird and Coghill, 1885.

'The Coopers' Hall,' Dorothy Vitner, *Western Daily Press*, 1962.

National Maritime Museum, ADM/C/366, 371, 706.

National Maritime Museum, ADM/C/407.

The British Museum MS. 24098 fol. 27b.

The British Museum MS. 18851 fol. 1.

CHAPTER TWELVE

Everyday Life in Colonial America, L. B. Wright, p. 95, 1965.

Woodland Crafts in Britain, H. L. Eldin, p. 72, 1949.

Catalogue of Coopers' Tools, Loftus Ltd. London 19th. century.

Story of Whitbreads, p. 38, 1947.

A Short History of Technology, Derry and Williams, p. 64, 1960.

The Cooperage Handbook, Hankerson, 1950.

The Coopers' Company and Craft, G. Elkington, 1933.

The Coopers' Company, J. F. Firth, 1848.

A Short History of the Coopers Company of London, Foster, p. 71, 1944.

A History of the Aberdeen Incorporated Trades, Ebenezer Bain, 1887.

Aberdeen; its Tradition and History, William Robbie, 1893.

The Incorporated Trades of Edinburgh, James Colston, 1891.

Fraternity of St. John of Leith . . . Documents 1550–1873, McInnes.

Museum of English Rural Life, Reading, 60/4483.

CHAPTER THIRTEEN

The Brewers Art, B. Brown, p. 16, 1948.

A Short History . . . Coopers of London, Foster, 1944.

The Coopers' Company, J. F. Firth, 1848.

The' Coopers' Company and Craft, G. Elkington, 1933.

The Cooperage Handbook, Hankerson, 1950.

Country Life and Craftsmen, Garry Hogg, p. 52, 1959.
The Craft of Coopering, Cork A.S., v. 49, 170, Coleman, 1944.
London Life in the Eighteenth Century, M. Dorothy George, 1925.
The Amorial Bearings of the Several Incorporate Companies of Newcastle on Tyne, James Walker and M. A. Richardson, 1824.
Guilds, Cornelius Walford, 1888.
Demon Gin, D. C. Paton, 1970.
King of Gin, David Jermyn, 1969.
The British Museum, MS. 32,922. BM/38.
The Hastings Fishing Museum.
The National Maritime Museum, ADM/C/705, 408, 366, 377.
Record Office, Bristol.

CHAPTER FOURTEEN

The Story of Whitbreads, p. 21, 1947.
The Coopers' Company and Craft, Elkington, 1933.
The History of Technology, vol. 3, p. 128, Jenkins and Salaman, 1958.
The Craft of Coopering, J. C. Coleman, Cork Arch. Society, vol. 49 No. 170, 1944.
The Noted Breweries of Great Britain and Ireland, A. Barnard, 1889.
Dionysus, Edward Hyams, p. 287, 1965.
National Maritime Museum, ADM/C/707, 706, 708. Order in Council 1/2/1813.
Royal Navy Historical Records. Nineteenth century Admiralty Instr.
Report of a trial taken in shorthand by Mr I. Cooke for the Port of London Authority.
Record Office Bristol.
Mr E. J. Hodder, Cooper of Bristol. Correspondence with author.
Friends of Humanity Centenary Pamphlet.
A History of English Ale and Beer, Monkton, p. 154, 1966.
The Sheffield Cooperage ⎱ Private correspondence with author.
David Roberts Cooperage ⎰
Samuel Kilby and Sons Cooperage, Banbury—Notes.
Bedfordshire Directories 1853, 1871 and 1910.
Cassey Directory 1862.
Kelly Directory 1894.
Guiness' Brewery in the Irish Economy, Lunch and Vaisey, p. 201, 202, 228, 1960.
J. & W. Burman's Cooperage, Burton on Trent. Conversations with author.

CHAPTER FIFTEEN

The Coopers' Company and Craft, Elkington, 1933.

China at Work, Rudolf P. Hommel.

A History of English Ale and Beer, H. A. Monkton, p. 23, 1966.

They Struck Oil, Hildegard Dolson, 1959.

The Coopers Federation of Great Britain and Ireland Annual Report 1951.

Port of London Authority Magazine, Article by Col. Oram.

George Gorrod, Deacon Convener and Cooper, Aberdeen. Conversation with author.

Henry Sutton, Great Yarmouth. Conversations with author.

Ministry of Fisheries, Lowestoft, Paper of 20–10–50.

The Yarmouth Mercury.

Mr Alexander Robertson. Correspondence with author.

Agreement between the Herring Trade Assn. and the Transport and General Workers Union, Coopers Section, March 1963.

Brewers Society Returns to the Timber Control, Board of Trade.

Acknowledgements

I wish first to thank Mr R. A. Salaman, without whose encouragement and generous help I would never have written this book. Mr James Dyer, Head of the History Department, Putteridge Bury College of Education, was also instrumental in that his infectious enthusiasm for history (and this book was begun as a dissertation for a Certificate of Education) had the effect of turning students into budding historians. I am also in his debt for some of the drawings and for reading the three chapters of early history.

I would next like to thank all my fellow coopers who have so generously given me of their time: Mr E. H. Pettengall, General Secretary, National Trade Union of Coopers; Mr David Roberts, Mr A. Robertson, Yarmouth; Mr E. J. Hodder, Bristol; Mr George Gorrod, Aberdeen; Mr W. Lloyd, Swansea; Mr J. and Mr W. Burman and Mr Oldham of Burton; Mr A. Hall, Mr Novic, London; The Sheffield Cooperage (Mr L. Wilson); Mr James Tilley, Leith; Mr Smith, Mr Skinner of Invergordon, and a host of others whose names escape me, and also to apologize for not having had the pleasure of seeing many more. I must thank Mr James Whitton, Secretary of the East and North of Scotland District Joint Industrial Council of the Cooperage Industry, for documents which he has lent to me. Mr Blakeman of Keillers, Dundee, Mr C. M. C. Newton of Ind Coope Ltd., Guildford, Henry Sutton of Yarmouth, Mr Leslie Gould of the *Yarmouth Mercury*, Mr W. L. Gates of Putteridge Bury College, Whitbreads of Luton and many other people have been most helpful in supplying me with information and material.

Museums, record offices and libraries up and down the country have tolerated my searching. These include the British Museum; the Science Museum; the Maritime Museum; the Guildhall Library; Record Office; Port of London Authority; the Yarmouth Fishing Museum; the Hastings Fishing Museum; the Norwich Reference Library; the Luton Museum; the Bedford Record Office; the Coventry Record Office; the York Reference Library; the Museum of English Rural Life, Reading;

the City Museum, Reading; the Record Office, Bristol; Art Gallery, Bristol; Bodleian Library, Oxford; Ashmolean Museum, Oxford; The Manchester Museum; Tribunal Museum, Glastonbury; Mitchell Library, Glasgow; Newcastle Reference Library; Edinburgh Reference Library; Fort William Folk Museum; Thurso Folk Museum; Aberdeen Reference Library; Perth Reference Library; Dundee Reference Library; Railway Museum, York; Jewry Wall Museum, Leicester; the Devizes Museum; Tullie House Museum, Carlisle; Liverpool City Museums, and others.

Lastly I would like to thank my family, who have shown great patience in accompanying me on so many of my journeys.

ILLUSTRATIONS AND DRAWINGS

I am indebted to Mr R. A. Salaman for Plates 1 and 4, taken at the St Albans City Museum. Plates 5, 6, 8, 10, 11, 13, 14, 15, 17, 18, 19, 21 and 99 are from the Tickenhill Collection, the proprietors of which I thank most sincerely. The Museum of English Rural Life, Reading were kind enough to supply me with plates 7, 9, 22, 23, 79 and 84. Plates 27, 28, 30, 57, 64, 85 and 89 are printed by permission of the Keeper of Printed Books, Bodleian Library, Oxford. I am indebted to the Invergordon Distillery for allowing me to take the photograph at plate 29, and to Messrs. J. & W. Burman of Burton for their kind co-operation in letting me take the photographs at plates 31 to 37. The Ashmolean Museum at Oxford supplied plates 51 and 61. Plates 52, 54, 63, 71, 74, 75, 76, 88 and 90 are from the British Museum, London. Plate 58 is from the Reading City Museum. I wish to thank the Director, Museums and Art Gallery, Leicester for permission to print plates 53 and 70. The Keeper of Archaeology, City of Liverpool Museums, Dorothy Slow, supplied plates 59 and 60. Plate 62 is from the Museum of Devizes, Wiltshire. Plate 69 is from the Weald and Downland Museum, West Dean, Near Chichester, Sussex. Plates 72 and 73 are from J. F. Firth's History of the Coopers' Company, and I should like to thank the Assistant Clerk to the Worshipful Company of Coopers and the Luton Public Library for help in obtaining the book. Plate 80 is printed by courtesy of the Trustees of the British Science Museum, London. The Heidelberg Castle Authorities supplied plate 81. Plate 82 is printed by permission of the Directors of the City Art Gallery, Bristol. Mr Reece Winstone supplied plate 86. Plate 87 is from the archives of the *Daily Telegraph*, and plate 95 from the archives of the *Daily Express*. Plate 91 is from the Centenary Booklet of the Bristol Friends of Humanity Society kindly lent me by Mr E. J. Hodder of Bristol. The Hulton Picture Library supplied plate 92. Plates 96 and 97 came from *The Yarmouth Mercury*. Lastly I should like to thank the Keeper of the Tullie House Museum, Carlisle, from whence came plate 104.

I am grateful to Mr James Dyer for his drawing of figures 3, 4, 5, 6, 7, 8, 10, 11, 12, 14, 48, 49, 50, 51, 52, 53 and 54, to James Kilby for drawing figure 1, and to Miss Carol Tarrant for her artistry in figures 69 and 74.

I would lastly like to thank those people and Institutions from whose work, possessions and documents the drawings were made: Mr R. A. Salaman for figure 18; The Archives du Musee, Wallone, for figures 22, 23, 24, 25, 26 and 27; The Bodleian Library for figures 28, 29, 30, 31, 32, 33, 34, 35, 36 and 37; The Yarmouth Fishing Museum for figure 38; Piggot's *Ancient Europe*, 1965, for figure 49; Quibell's *Tomb of Hesy*, 1913, for figure 52; Newbury's *Beni Hasan*, 1893, for figure 53; The Manchester Museum for figure 54; The Tribunal Museum, Glastonbury for figure 55; Bulleid and Gray's *The Glastonbury Lake Village* for figures 56, 57 and 58; Elkington's *The Coopers Company and Craft* for figures 59, 69, 73 and 74; *Mind Alive Encyclopedia* for figure 60; G. Bersu and H. Hencken in the 'Ulster Journal of Archaeology' for figure 61; George Bass's *Archaeology under Water* for figure 62; The Bibliotheque Nationale, Paris for figure 65; The Mitchell Library, Glasgow for figure 66; The Newcastle Reference Library for figure 67; The Aberdeen Reference Library for figure 76; The Directors of Whitbread's Brewery for figures 77 and 81; The Fort William Folk Museum for figure 79; The Directors of Ind Coope Ltd. for figure 80; Mr M. S. Longuet-Higgins for figure 82; and Rudolf P. Hommel's *China at Work* for figure 86.

Index